GOD IN YOU, TO YOU, AND FOR YOU

Marilyn Hickey

WORD OF FAITH
LEADERSHIP AND BIBLE INSTITUTE

**All Scripture quotations
from the King James Version
of the Bible unless otherwise stated**

ISBN 0-914307-13-4

Printed in the United States of America
Copyright © 1983 WORD OF FAITH PUBLISHING
PO Box 819000, Dallas, Texas 75381

Table of Contents

Marilyn Hickey's captivating style of delivery, coupled with a remarkable insight into the original meanings of Hebrew and Greek words, has elevated her to an undisputed position as "the people's theologian"!

Fascinating her reading audience with rich illustrations from Bible and her own personal life, Marilyn is recognized as one of the world's most entertaining and thought-provoking Biblical teachers in the world today! Her spiritual insight will make you desire and earnestly yearn to discover the blessings which God has custom-designed especially for you! Marilyn will lead you into the glorious experience of knowing Jesus in His majestic fullness. Jesus Christ is the Lord of Marilyn's life, and she eagerly shares her dynamic revelations of Him on radio and television stations around the world, as she fulfills the prophecy which God gave her. Hearing God's call, Marilyn enthusiastically said, "Here I am; Send me!" God gave her a task that would seem staggering in the natural but exceedingly POSSIBLE in the Spirit, and that was to "COVER THE EARTH WITH THE WORD!"

Marilyn's deep sensitivity to the voice of the Holy Spirit will inspire you to reach out for all of the blessings and power that God has given you as your rightful inheritance. Marilyn will motivate you to use your "sword of the Spirit," the Word, to lift yourself above your circumstances and "sit in heavenly places in Christ Jesus!!!"

FOREWARD

Elohim...El Shaddai...Jehovah...Adonai.... One day I found myself wondering why God had so many names. So I asked Him, and He said, "Marilyn, those names express every aspect of the relationship which I desire to have with you, and with all of My people. Each name presents a different aspect of My personality and provision."

As I began studying the names of God, He revealed something which is rather extraordinary: your self image will be complete when you realize the complete image of Who God wants to be **in you!** All that he is, and all that He has ever been--every dimension of His amazing personality awaits, ready to reach fulfillment in you; ready to complete your self image! By this study's end, you will begin seeing the impact of having been made in the image of God. You will be on your way to a walk with Him that is more flourishing and fruitful than you ever before imagined!

Chapter 1

ELOHIM

The very first title of God that you encounter in the Bible is found in Genesis 1:1.

In the beginning God created the heaven and the earth. (Genesis 1:1)

The Hebrew translation for the word **God** is actually "El," or "Elohim." Fascinating in its translation, this name is one of God's more frequently-occurring titles in the Bible; it shows up over 2,500 times! It must be important that we understand its meaning.

El is the root word of "Elohim," and it describes God's **greatness and glory**; it displays God's **power and sovereignty.** Although this word is comprised of only two letters, it offers a glimpse into the depth of the Hebrew language—a language of pictures.

Consider the name **Elohim**, which extends the scope of El's root meaning. **Elohim** brings forth a new dimension to the God of power: He becomes the God Who **creates!** Two facets of God make up the word "Elohim" so far:

    1. Total power and might, and complete sovereignty;

    2. Complete creativity.

Notice that in the Bible's very first verse, God was shown as the Creator! In using the name Elohim, Genesis 1:1 makes the statement that tremendous, unimaginable power is involved in the force of God's creativity! Elohim, in His mighty power and awesome creativity, caused our vast universe to exist.

> *Through faith we understand that the worlds were framed by the word of God, so that things which are seen were not made of things which do appear.* (Hebrews 11:3)

God's name, Elohim, is amazing in itself, but it bears another striking characteristic which makes it even **more** distinctive: the Hebrew ending for Elohim is plural!

Why? Because it describes the divine trinity of the Godhead: Father, Son, and Holy Spirit. No singular word could adequately describe this element of God's personality.

Several places throughout the Bible confirm this plurality. Genesis 1 says this about the creation of the first man, Adam:

> *26 And God said, Let us make man in **our** image, after **our** likeness...*
>
> *27 So God created man in his own image, in the image of God created he him; male and female created he them.* (Genesis 1:26-27)

God the Father, Jesus the Son, and the Holy Spirit were all involved in the powerful creative process which is described in Genesis 1. Genesis 1 shows that the Holy Spirit was present.

2 ...And the Spirit of God moved upon the face of the waters.

3 And God said, Let there be light: and there was light. (Genesis 1:2-3)

Why was the Holy Spirit moving upon the face of the waters? Because He was preparing to create!

Jesus was also an active and present part of creation.

For by him were all things created, that are in heaven, and that are in earth, visible and invisible, whether they be thrones, or dominions, or principalities, or powers: all things were created by him, and for him. (Colossians 1:16)

Active, present, full of creative power: Elohim! Father, Son, and Holy Spirit.

This increases the impact of Jesus' shocking statement to the religious men of His day: "Before Abraham was, I Am." What an exciting, infinite personality!

I like this analogy. God is the Architect; Jesus is the Builder; and the Holy Spirit is He who breathes the life of God into the structure. Elohim: Those Who are mighty and powerful; Those Who are creative and sovereign.

Yet, there is another facet to the Elohim, making Him an active part of His creation. It is Elohim who makes covenants with those whom He created! Later, you will study the name Jehovah, the name in which God reveals His ways; Elohim is the name in which God reveals His

power. It is this very power and creativity which allows God Himself to enter into covenant relationship with you and me.

The apostle Paul had a revelation of Elohim.

For I am not ashamed of the gospel of Christ: for it is the power of God unto salvation to every one that believeth; to the Jew first, and also to the Greek. (Romans 1:16)

What was Paul saying? He was saying, "God's covenant of salvation with you and me **is** His power!" Don't ever speak lightly of the gospel--God's covenant with us--for that is His power which gave us eternal life; His power which saved us now and forever! Our covenant-making Elohim sustains all that He created through His own might. Throughout Genesis, whenever God created, He **spoke** first; then came the manifestation of His power.

Naturally, Elohim loved His creation. He desired to preserve it. But, although God was protective toward the people of His creation, they seemed to only get better and better at being worse and worse! And as the people sinned, they separated themselves further away from their Creator. Although God is merciful, He is also holy and righteous. Sin was (and still is) offensive to Him, and something had to be done before these people destroyed themselves. Elohim observed this growing sinfulness spread like cancer as several generations passed by.

As man continued in this downhill pattern, God began to notice a man named Enoch. Enoch wasn't outstanding in his hunger for God, and his life was fairly uneventful until he reached age 65. But then something happened that turned his life around. Enoch's wife bore

a child, and God told Enoch, *"Name that baby Methuselah"*--which means, *"I've had enough of this sinfulness, so when that child dies, the flood will come upon
the earth."*

Surely no child received the tender, loving care that
Methuselah had! Enoch lived in a day without modern
medicine. Death was a frequent visitor, and it frequently
took small babies and children, who lacked resistance to
disease. You can imagine Enoch's shock: *"If this baby
dies, the deluge will come and totally destroy the earth.
Take good care of him!"*

As Enoch lovingly cared for Methuselah, something
began to happen within him. Enoch's heart somehow responded to his Creator. Enoch began to serve the Lord.
For 300 years he built a relationship with God, walking
and increasing in faith. Finally something really tremendous took place.

*And Enoch walked with God: and he was not;
for God took him.* (Genesis 5:24)

One day, Enoch was going about his usual routine,
increasing in faith, and all of a sudden, God just reached
down and carried him out of this life, across into life eternal! That's what **translate** means: "to carry across." Hebrews 11:5 says Enoch was translated by faith!
Meanwhile, Methuselah was still alive, growing older,
probably keeping people on pins and needles. They knew
the day was coming when the floods would arrive.

Although Enoch had been walking closely with God,
the same thing can't be said about the other people of his
generation. Their sinfulness vexed God continually. Yet
Methuselah lived longer than any other person recorded

5

in the Bible --969 years! His life was tremendously long for one reason: God kept extending His mercy and grace, hoping to preserve His creation! He loved those people, and did not want to destroy them.

Methuselah had a child named Lamech, and one of Lamech's sons was Noah. Notice the family lines. When you enter into a covenant with God, His promises are unto **your seed**, and their seed, and to as many as the Lord your God shall call!

One day God spoke to Noah.

And God said unto Noah, The end of all flesh is come before me; for the earth is filled with violence through them; and, behold, I will destroy them with the earth. (Genesis 6:13)

God proceeded to give Noah directions for building the ark, and Noah obeyed. Over the years, people began taking God's warning for granted. I would have thought that when Noah started building, they'd have said, "Oh no! Methuselah's dead, and God is going to send that flood He warned us about!"

The people did something completely opposite-- they scoffed at Noah. They'd had almost one thousand years in which to repent. But, although Noah preached to the people about God's intentions, they rebelled.

God always warns His people ahead of time when judgment is coming. He wants to give everyone a chance to repent first.

I pictured Noah in my mind, out there building this huge ark; and then the Lord began revealing Noah's faith to me. Noah had tremendous faith! Especially so, considering the fact that rain had never before fallen upon the

6

earth!

Noah built that ark to comply with God's specifications, and it took 120 years to accomplish it. Just imagine having people harass you for that long. He had every physical reason to stop in the 80th year and say, "I've had enough of building this while everybody else laughs! God, this is ridiculous--I mean, I've never even seen rain before, and here You have me preaching that there's going to be a flood! I quit!"

But Noah didn't give up. He held fast to the confidence of God's Word, and kept building.

35 Cast not away therefore your confidence, which hath great recompence of reward.

36 For ye have need of patience, that, after ye have done the will of God, ye might receive the promise. (Hebrews 10:35-36)

Noah received a big reward for his patience--he had **finished** the will of God! He and his family were spared, and the seed parts of the earth were saved, so that it, too, could be replenished.

When God calls you to accomplish something, don't quit! God could have just said, "I've had it; I'm destroying this whole earth!" But He didn't say that. Noah could have quit very easily--but he didn't. And you should never give up, because you have been created in God's image, and God doesn't give up!

After having finished God's will, Noah and his family were spared. When the flooding was over and the ark rested on top of Mount Ararat, God showed Himself again to Noah--as **Elohim**, the God Who makes covenants! God first spoke as Jehovah, and told Noah to make a sacrifice

7

unto Him. Noah brought forth the animals and obeyed, making a sweet-smelling sacrifice unto the Lord.

Then something beautiful happened.

11 And I will establish my covenant with you; neither shall all flesh be cut off any more by the waters of a flood; neither shall there any more be a flood to destroy the earth.

12 And God said, This is the token of the covenant which I make between me and you and every living creature that is with you, for perpetual generations:

13 I do set my bow in the cloud, and it shall be for a token of a covenant between me and the earth. (Genesis 9:11-13)

Elohim showed Himself in two ways: He **created** a rainbow by His mighty power; and He made a **covenant** with Noah. That rainbow was God's sign which told Noah, "I will never flood the earth again," and the rainbow should still remind you and me of that same covenant. God, mighty and powerful, wants to tenderly protect His creation. So when you see a rainbow, think of Elohim! Think of God who enters into everlasting agreements with His people.

God made a covenant with Abraham, also. The first time He ever spoke to Abraham (then, he was still called **Abram**) is recorded in Genesis 12. When God first spoke to him, He used two names: **Jehovah** and **Elohim**.

1 Now the LORD had said unto Abram, get thee out of thy country, and from thy kindred, and from thy father's house, unto a land that I will shew thee:

2 And I will make of thee a great nation, and I will bless thee and make thy name great; and thou shalt be a blessing:

3 And I will bless them that bless thee, and curse him that curseth thee: and in thee shall all families of the earth be blessed. (Genesis 12:1-3)

This is how God revealed Himself to Abraham--as a God of blessing! He was speaking as Jehovah. You will study the name "Jehovah" later, but these few verses will allow you to differentiate God as Elohim--the covenant God of might.

2 And Abram said, Lord GOD, what wilt thou give me, seeing I go childless, and the steward of my house is this Eliezer of Damascus?

3 And Abram said, Behold, to me thou hast given no seed: and, lo, one born in my house is mine heir.

4 And, behold, the word of the LORD came unto him, saying, This shall not be thine heir; but he that shall come forth out of thine own bowels shall be thine heir.

5 And he brought him forth abroad, and said, Look now toward heaven, and tell the stars, if thou be able to number them: and he said unto him, So shall thy seed be. (Genesis 15:2-5)

God was covenanting with Abram to give him a child. When Abram said, "Lord, God," he was saying, "I know Your ways, for You have revealed them to me. But I want a covenant with You, for You are able to give me a child."

It is in this same chapter that Elohim makes a covenant with Abram!

When God first spoke to Abram, He commanded him to do three things. But Abram obeyed only two of them in the beginning. He was told to:

1. leave his country.
2. leave his relatives.
3. travel to a land which God would lead him to.

Abraham did leave his country for the land of promise, but he did one thing wrong--he took relatives with him.

Accompanying Abram was a nephew named **Lot**, and his father, whose name was **Terah**. Terah literally means "delay," and he really created a delay for Abram. God wanted to make a covenant with Abram, who was to become the "Father of faith," but He could not make the agreement while his eyes were on family, instead of God.

On the way to the land of promise, Terah, who was very old and tired, needed to stop. Abram, Lot, and Terah halted their journey at a place called **Haran**, which means "dry and parched." There they stayed for almost two years, until Terah finally died.

God told Abram, "Don't take your relatives." But because Abram did things his own way, he ended up in a dry, parched place where he couldn't hear from God.

We are supposed to love, honor, and obey our parents--that is a commandment from God Himself. But we are not to revere our relatives over the Word of God! That's when trouble comes. Let God have the very first place in your life. When you do, your spiritual walk will never become dry and parched; it will always be refreshing.

Because Abram had delayed for almost two years, when he finally did reach the promised land, there was a famine going on. Imagine how discouraging it must have been for him. After two years of delay in this desert land called Haran, he finally got to his destination, and things weren't any better there! In addition, he hadn't heard the voice of God for two years. He probably wondered whether he would ever hear it again!

Many people wonder why God rarely speaks to them, when they haven't obeyed His first instruction. Silence may be God's way of saying, "You haven't finished what I asked you to complete. When you fully obey My first Words, I'll speak to you again--but not until then!" It took Abram a while to get the hint.

Now in the land of promise, Abram built an altar between **Bethel**, which means "the house of God," and **Hai**, which means "a place of ruin."

I would have built the temple right inside "the house of God." But Abram was just beginning to walk by faith. Perhaps he wasn't quite ready to build in Bethel yet.

The major activity with which Abram concerned himself during his lifetime was building altars. He was a man who communed regularly with God and Jehovah. He highly esteemed the covenant God of might. One really positive point in Abram's story is that, although there were delays, God always overcame them.

Be encouraged by the accounts of those men of faith who paved our way. We have the opportunity to learn from their mistakes, and to be encouraged by how God divinely overcame the flaws of their humanity.

Abram and his wife, whose name was Sarai, took Lot and traveled to Egypt to escape the famine. When they returned, Abram's altar had been destroyed, so he rebuilt it. Then Abram took his family and moved to a place between **Mamre**, which means "fatness," and **Hebron**, which means "fellowship." Perhaps this was Abram's way of saying, "Devil, you can't try to destroy what I've built! I'll just rebuild it. And not only that, but I'll build a second, even **better** altar."

Abram's new altar is significant, because it shows that his communion with God was flourishing. But Abram was still having trouble with unbelief concerning God's promise about his descendants.

He and Sarai still had not had any children. Abram probably thought, "Just in case I don't receive children from God, I can raise my nephew Lot as my own child." He was trying to play it safe, just in case God didn't come through on His part of the bargain.

Eventually though, Abram and Lot had no choice-- they had to separate. And it turned out to be the best thing they did! They both had herdmen who were tending flocks, and soon these herdmen began to have great disagreements among themselves.

One day, Abram confronted Lot.

8 And Abram said unto Lot, Let there be no strife, I pray thee, between me and thee, and between my herdmen and thy herdmen; for we be brethren.

9 Is not the whole land before thee? separate thyself, I pray thee, from me: If thou wilt take

*the left hand, then I will go to the right: or if
thou depart to the right hand, then I will go to
the left.* (Genesis 13:8-9)

Abram really exercised his godly qualities. He didn't
say, "Well, Lot, since I'm older, you'd better honor me.
I'll take the best portion of land."

No! He said, "Lot, there are two sections of land: one
to my right, and one to my left. **You choose** whichever
you prefer. I'll take the one that is left."

Many people who read this instantly think, "Abram
was being humble; he didn't want to take the best for himself." But that is not the case.

Abram knew **Elohim**--God almighty! Abram knew
Elohim--the God Who made covenants. It didn't matter
to him which land he chose, because he knew, no matter
where he lived, God would protect him. By faith, Abram
was saying, "It doesn't matter what my circumstances say.
I know Elohim, and He rules over circumstances!"

When Abram gave Lot the choice between lands, Lot
immediately looked around, and he saw two things.

*And Lot lifted up his eyes, and beheld all the
plain of Jordan, that it was well watered every
where, before the LORD destroyed Sodom and
Gomorrah, even as the garden of the LORD,
like the land of Egypt, as thou comest unto
Zoar.* (Genesis 13:10)

Then Lot said, "Abram, I'll take that nice, well-
watered plain over there. You can have the mountainous
region."

Their decisions having been made, Lot and Abram
separated. Abram and Sarai went off to their arid, moun-

tainous area. And when they got there, what do you think happened? God spoke to him again!

*14 And the LORD said unto Abram, **after that Lot was separated from him**, Lift up now thine eyes, and look from the place where thou art northward, and southward, and eastward, and westward:*

15 For all the land which thou seest, to thee will I give it, and to thy seed for ever. (Genesis 13:14-15)

It must have been wonderful to hear from God again. And finally, Abram knew the time was near to draw into a covenant with Almighty God. When God spoke this to him, Abram did not merely look around casually and say, "This, for me? Oh, God, how nice!"

The Bible says that Abram **lifted up** his eyes! I believe he lifted up his eyes and received a **vision**--he saw what God saw, and it was a vision of faith!

When Abram looked northward, I think he saw the entire northern part of the Holy Land. Southward, Abram saw far, far beyond the mountain that blocked his view. Eastward and westward, what do you think Abram saw? He probably saw all the way to the Mediterranean Sea, and over into Jordan! Abram's relatives were out of the way-- now he could focus his eyes on God. But after God told Abram, "Lift up your eyes," He told him something else.

Arise, walk through the land in the length of it and in the breadth of it; for I will give it unto thee. (Genesis 13:17)

A faith vision isn't enough. You have to do more than just have a vision--you have to live it! You must **walk** it!

14

I used to know of a man who would sit on his porch in his rocking chair, saying, "I wish I had a million dollars. I wish I had a million dollars."

Do you think he ever got it?

No! You don't obtain a million dollars while sitting in a rocking chair. You don't get things by wishing for them. Some people have the vision, but they don't have the action that goes with it.

God told Abram, "You have to act on this vision! Walk through the land; I will give you the land that you tread upon."

I think Abram was the world's first jogger. He jogged north, south, east, and west. I can imagine the Canaanites talking as Abram jogged by. "Who is that man who just jogged down the road?"

"I don't know, but I saw him going the other direction yesterday."

Abram was running as the man who would possess the land. He was thinking of God's Words, which said that his seed's seed would possess the land! Running along, I'm sure Abram was saying, "This is mine; this is mine..." as he prepared himself to enter into a covenant-relationship with God.

But after Abram claimed that land, something happened--and it didn't surprise me a bit! A wicked king named Chedorlaomer roused up a group of other kings, and they came down from Elam (now Iran) with trouble on their minds. When they reached the cities of Sodom and Gomorrah--land upon which Abram had trod--they attacked, and took off with both people and possessions. They even captured Lot, Abram's nephew.

The devil will try to steal what you've claimed! When you claim something, and tread upon the ground of God's Word by speaking His promises, you had better prepare for battle. Some people stake their claims, but as soon as the enemy says, "You can't have that," they'll lie down and play dead! Of course the devil comes to steal--Jesus told you that he would. but you don't need to take it!

Abram wasn't about to play the enemy's game--he really got bold. Abram said, "They can't do this! I trod upon this land, and it's mine. So I won't put up with the enemy's tricks."

I wondered, "How could one man be so bold?" But then I realized, **it's because he knew Elohim--the God of covenant relationships.** He knew God would not give him land if he couldn't **keep** it. That land was for his seed's seed. Abram banded together a group of men, and they went up to Elam and took everything back-- **everything**!

Some people say, "They're going to blow up the whole earth with these nuclear weapons!"

They'll never do it, because God is bigger and mightier and more powerful than any bomb that man has ever made. God is not going to have His earth blown up until He is ready to finish it the way He wants to. He will do it by fire, but I don't believe it will be by an atomic bomb. I don't accept that, because God knows how to take care of His creation--and He has done so for a long time.

God knows how to take care of you, because you have entered into a covenant relationship with Him. How do I know? Because by faith, you're the seed of Abraham, and He told Abraham, "Surely blessing I will bless you, and multiplying I will multiply you." He is your covenant making God. He is the God of might and power. He put Abram over, in his situation, and gave him might and power to win; **and He will give you might and power to win, also.**

18 In the same day the LORD made a covenant with Abram, saying, Unto thy seed have I given this land, from the river of Egypt unto the great river, the river Euphrates:

19 The Kenites, and the Kenizzites, and the Kadmonites,

20 And the Hittites, and the Perizzites, and the Rephaims,

21 And the Amorites, and the Canaanites, and the Girgashites, and the Jebusites. (Genesis 15:18-21)

The Lord God entered into a covenant with Abram. He said, "We have a relationship between ourselves, and I'm giving you all of this land."

What would it take for Abram and Sarai to realize the impact of having a covenant with Almighty God? At this point, all they seemed to realize was that they were supposed to have seed (children) and they still didn't have any! Abram must have thought, "It's going to take a lot of might and power to keep this covenant, because we're way past childbearing years!"

When Abram was 99 years old, and Sarai was 89, God finally told them that they would have children. He also changed their names. Abram became "Abraham," which means "Father of a multitude," and Sarai became "Sarah," which means "Princess of many nations."

How could this be? The Bible says, when God first changed Abram's name, he laughed out loud; he couldn't believe it! And when Sarai heard God telling Abram that he would have a child, how do you think she reacted? She laughed too. Abram's divine Visitor said, "Sarai laughed," and she was so embarrassed that she denied it.

They did have a child, and God pre-named the child **Isaac**--which means "laughter." Abram and Sarai may have both laughed, but God had the last laugh! Then, in Hebrews 11, Isaac's birth is spoken of. It says that Sarah received the strength to have that child **by faith**. It took more than just Abraham's faith to have seed; they had to be in agreement! Hebrews 11 says that Sarah received strength; and the word for strength is **dunamis**, or "miracle-working power." Where did that miracle-working power come from? It came from Elohim, the God of might and power!

You need to have a renewed image of the God of might and power--the God Who is more than able to put you over in any difficulty! If God (Elohim) is for you, who can possibly be against you? No one! Elohim is more powerful than anything else that exists, and He is on your side.

God wants you to rely on Him as your source of power and might. He wants to be Elohim **to** you, **for** you, and **in** you. Right now, no matter what the circumstances may be in your life, will you let Him? Let Him renew your spirit, your mind, your body, your emotions, and your image. As you go through your Bible, from now on, every time you see the word "God," think, "That's Elohim, the God of might and power--and He's **my** God!" Praise the Lord!

Elohim - Here are some scripture references which refer to God as Elohim. When you need His power and might at work in your life, read through them and refresh your vision of His covenant with you. But you don't have to wait until a crisis! Any time is the best time to look through these scriptures.

2: I will say of the LORD, he is my refuge and my fortress: my God; in him will I trust.

3 Surely he shall deliver thee from the snare of the fowler, and from the noisome pestilence.

4 He shall cover thee with his feathers, and under his wings shalt thou trust; his truth shall be thy shield and buckler. (Psalm 91:2-4)

38 And they shall be my people, and I will be their God:

39 And I will give them one heart, and one way, that they may fear me for ever, for the good of them, and of their children after them:

40 And I will make an everlasting covenant with them, that I will not turn away from them, to do them good; but I will put my fear in their hearts, that they shall not depart from me. (Jeremiah 32:38-40)

And he (Solomon) said, LORD God of Israel, there is no God like thee, in heaven above, or on earth beneath, who keepest covenant and mercy with thy servants that walk before thee with all their heart. (1st Kings 8:23)

1 Be merciful unto me, O God, be merciful unto me: for my soul trusteth in thee: yea, in the shadow of thy wings will I make my refuge, until these calamities be overpast.

2 I will cry unto God most high; unto God that performeth all things for me.

3 He shall send from heaven, and save me from the reproach of him that would swallow me up. Selah. God shall send forth his mercy and his truth. (Psalm 57:1-3)

Chapter 2

JEHOVAH

Derived from the Hebrew word **chavah**, which means "to live," the name **Jehovah** is literally full of life! It is written into the King James Version of the Bible as **LORD**, and it means "to be," or "being."

Now that you have seen God as all-powerful, mighty Elohim, Who desires a covenant with those whom He created, you will love meeting Him as Jehovah--the Revealing One! This name of God brings Him forth in a very personal way, and it is the very essence of the present tense.

When Adam and Eve talked to God in the Garden, they did not call Him Jehovah; they called Him Elohim, for they did not know a personal, intimate walk with the Lord.

Has the Lord ever spoken to you? He has spoken often to me through divine impressions in my spirit. Sweet and precious in their messages, I have known they were from the Lord--that is, Jehovah, the Revealing One.

I remember a specific time when He characterized this wonderful side of His personality as I was praying. I said, "Lord, it's such a privilege to live for You."

And He said, "Marilyn, you don't live only **for** Me-- you live **with** Me!"

Jehovah--He is the One Who makes Himself known to you as your intimate, personal God. He walks with you, always in the present tense, and He will never leave nor forsake you. The more you grow in this relationship with Him, the more of Himself He will reveal to you.

Jehovah also denotes the unchangeability of God. *"In him there is no variableness nor shadow of turning."* Psalm 102:27 reads, *"But thou art the same, and thy years shall have no end."* Jehovah is the One Who is now, and always has been. This is the God of life, the God of eternity!

In our study of this name, we will study the life of Moses in Exodus. Moses was called by God to deliver His people from Egypt. Moses' family was aware of his calling, and they were a family of faith. They were also enslaved to the Egyptian people. But through miraculous circumstances, Moses grew up in the Pharaoh's palace, and was trained to be the next Pharaoh in line--quite a comfortable set of circumstances! To the natural eye, it probably looked to Moses' parents as if he couldn't possibly be a deliverer of the Hebrews. He had it made; why would he want to deliver the Israelites from the hand of the Egyptians?

But God will deal with someone until He wins! And God dealt with Moses. At forty, Moses finally decided, since God had called him to deliver the Israelites, he may as well get on with it.

Did you ever try to help God?

I know we all have at times, and that was what Moses did. He got emotional one day when he saw an Egyptian man beating one of the Israelites, and Moses ran out and killed the Egyptian.

That really created trouble. The Egyptians were furious, and Moses had to flee for his life. Not only that, but they really cracked down on the Israelites; so the Israelites were enraged at Moses too!

Moses fled to a place called Midian. He lived in the desert for forty years, tending sheep. I've often wondered about what he did during those forty years. Some Bible scholars think he wrote the book of Job; and he very well could have. Some say he wrote Genesis, but I think Genesis was written with the rest of the Pentateuch on Mount Sinai.

God was using all of the experience Moses was having there in the desert, because he would later lead his people through a desert. Moses probably knew all about the desert after having lived there for forty years.

Moses also knew all about sheep--and people can be a lot like sheep. The prophet Isaiah said that we have all gone astray like sheep.

God is so economical! If you give Him half an opportunity, He will use everything in your life and turn it into glory for Him. I'm sure Moses did not expect God to turn his situation into a glorious one. In fact, I think he lost confidence that God would ever use him again.

Moses forgot that God plays until He wins. And when God wins, He wants to make you a winner, too! Every time you win, it credits God! Every time you have won in the past, it credited God.

The apostle Paul said it well: *"Now thanks be unto God, which always causeth us to triumph in Christ."* (2nd Corinthians 2:14) God wanted Moses to win, and He had set some high goals for Moses.

God has high goals for the lives of all of His people. Don't get jealous of other Christians when they do things well--you're a part of the same Body of Christ! Instead, support them. Say, "When you're doing well, so am I, because we're a part of the same Body!"

When I go to Oral Roberts University, or the City of Faith, I don't get jealous. I don't complain, "God, why did You use Oral, instead of me?"

No! I let that stimulate my faith, and I say, "Dear God! If you can do it for Oral Roberts, you can do it for Marilyn Hickey!"

Success is a credit to God's kingdom! Moses didn't have anyone around to stimulate his faith the way we can for each other. So God stepped into the scene with every intention of turning Moses into a winner, whether or not he was even aware of it.

One day, Moses was tending sheep near a place called Mount Horeb (Sinai), which means "fresh inspiration." Just think. God was getting ready to give Moses fresh inspiration, after forty years in the wilderness.

Have you ever felt like you've been in the wilderness for forty years? God can give you fresh inspiration, even if you've really blown it! He will always pick you up; He

24

will never put you down!

There was Moses, tending sheep, and all of a sudden he saw a burning bush which had a very unusual characteristic--the fire was not consuming it! Then God spoke to Moses from the fire.

4 ...God called unto him out of the midst of the bush, and said, Moses, Moses.

and Moses said, Here am I.

5 And he said, Draw not nigh hither: put off thy shoes from off thy feet, for the place whereon thou standest is holy ground. (Exodus 3:4-5)

What a shock! I don't think Moses had ever expected to hear the Lord again!

7 And the LORD said, I have surely seen the affliction of my people which are in Egypt, and have heard their cry by reason of their taskmasters; for I know their sorrows;

8 And I am come down to deliver them out of the hand of the Egyptians, and to bring them up out of that land unto a good land and a large, unto a land flowing with milk and honey; unto the place of the Canaanites, and the Hittites, and the Amorites, and the Perizzites, and the Hivites, and the Jebusites. (Exodus 3:7-8)

Basically, God was saying, *"Moses, you're still the man I want to use."*

Moses just about fell apart over it, too. He was eighty years old! Forty years ago he'd have said, "Don't you know that I am your deliverer?"

Now he was saying, "Who am I? I've blown it so badly!"

And now God was saying, *"You're ready to deliver."*

God majors in creating winners! He said, *"I will be with you and give you a token of My presence, Moses. You will go back and lead My people out of Egypt; and then you'll return to this mountain and serve Me."*

That was the mountain where God gave Moses the ten commandments; Mount Horeb is where Moses spent precious time with Jehovah, the Revealing One!

Moses said, "When I go to deliver the children of Israel, they're going to ask me Your Name--and I don't even know it!"

God told him, *"You just tell them thatI AM sent you."*

Who is I AM?

That's Jehovah, the One who revealed Himself to the children of Israel!

Not only was He revealing **Himself** to them, but also He was revealing His **plan** to deliver them from the Egyptians and lead them into the Promised Land. God didn't want Moses limiting Him with one name--He planned to be all that the children of Israel would need, so He was saying, *"I AM. I shall be everything to you!"*

And God said unto Moses, I AM THAT I AM: and he said, Thus shalt thou say unto the children of Israel, I AM hath sent me unto you. (Exodus 3:15)

Here God was revealing Himself as Jehovah--the One Who is the same yesterday, today, and forever! He was saying, *"I am Abraham's God, Isaac's God, Jacob's God, and I am YOUR God! Generations change, but I don't change, Moses."*

He revealed that Moses was to be the person who would deliver the Israelites from the hand of the Egyptians. But, although God may have been full of plans, Moses was full of excuses.

Moses said, "The elders of Israel aren't going to buy this, God. After all, look at what happened the last time."

God said, *"What's that in your hand?"*

"It's a rod, Lord."

"Throw it down on the ground."

...And he cast it on the ground, and it became a serpent; and Moses fled from before it. (Exodus 4:3)

God said, *"Pick it up, Moses, don't run from it!"*

Moses picked up the "serpent," and immediately it was a rod in his hand again! But, even though God told Moses, *"I will give that sign to the elders, and to Pharaoh,"* Moses was still skeptical. He just couldn't imagine himself as much of a deliverer. Then God said, *"If that isn't enough, Moses, I'll give you another sign."*

6 And the LORD said furthermore unto him, Put now thine hand into thy bosom. And he put his hand into his bosom: and when he took it out, behold, his hand was leprous as snow.

7 And he said, Put thine hand into thy bosom again. And he 'put his hand into his bosom again; and plucked it out of his bosom, and behold, it was turned again as his other flesh. (Exodus 4:6-7)

The first time Moses brought his hand out, it was leprous. God was telling him, *"Moses, you were led by the wrong motive to deliver when you killed that Egyptian man. You were trying to deliver by yourself, and you were not following Me as Jehovah. I had not yet revealed Myself to you. When you put your hand on your heart this time, your hand will be clean--just like your spiritual motive."*

This time, when Moses went forth to deliver, signs would accompany his calling.

God was overcoming all of Moses' arguments. Moses was still holding out, though. He said, "Lord, I just can't do it. I don't speak well enough."

When he said this, the Lord must have thought, *"That's not even true,"* because Acts 7:22 says that Moses was "mighty in word and deed." With the best of Egyptian training, Moses had been schooled for eloquent public speaking. Perhaps his exile in the desert had given him a bad self-image. Whatever the case, God was about fed up with excuses!

11 And the LORD said unto him, Who hath made man's mouth? or who maketh the dumb, or deaf, or the seeing, or the blind? have not I the LORD?

12 Now therefore go, and I will be with thy mouth, and teach thee what thou shalt say. (Exodus 4:11-12)

"Who made your mouth, anyway?" Isn't that a good reply? Jehovah had to remind Moses that He is also the powerful Creator, Elohim. And He told Moses, *"Look!*

If you're going to drag around, we'll get Aaron, your brother, to speak for you. Besides, all the men who sought your life are dead, so you don't have a thing to worry about."

That stripped away Moses' last excuse. He probably thought that he'd be facing people who wanted his head. Jehovah won him over, and, as it turned out, Aaron never did any of the speaking. Moses did all of it. After all, when the Lord God is on your side, who else do you need?

When Moses arrived in Egypt, God gave tremendous demonstrations of His power as Elohim. As Moses spoke the Word, and God was revealed as Jehovah--I AM, mighty works followed. Every plague upon Egypt was a judgment against an idol they worshipped. They worshipped the Nile river, and it was turned into blood. They worshipped a frog god called **Heki**, and mummified frogs, so God said, *"You like frogs? I'll give you lots of them!"*

The Egyptians also worshipped a sun god called **Ra**, so God plagued them with darkness. This darkness was very discriminating--it was only dark in Egypt; over in Goshen, where the Israelites lived, light still shone.

I'm sure that made the Pharaoh suspect that something was up. God was trying to win the Egyptians, as well as the Israelites--He loves the sinner, too! Those mighty signs were His way of saying, *"Your idols are wrong. Turn to Me."*

Finally, the Pharaoh's heart was turned, and he set the children of Israel free. I think a lot of the Egyptians were won over, also, because the Bible says that "a mixed multitude" followed Moses out of Egypt, into the wilderness.

But the trials weren't over yet.

God really took care of those people. Their shoes and garments didn't wear out, and they even had heating and air conditioning. A cloud cover by day, and a pillar of fire by night shielded them from scorching days and bitterly cold desert nights. God even acted as their military protection. Who else would part a body of water so that you could pass through without being harmed?

But how easily they seemed to forget. The children of Israel started to murmur, and that didn't go over well with either God bor Moses.

Exodus 31 describes many of the Israelites' experiences as they sojourned through the wilderness and arrived at Mount Horeb, where Moses had first heard God's voice from the burning bush.

God took Moses to the mountaintop and began speaking to him, and gave him the ten commandments. I also believe this is where God revealed Genesis to Moses, too. Moses wasn't just sitting idly up on the mountain for forty days, although a lot of people probably imagine that. I'm sure God kept him busy.

But while Moses was up on Mount Horeb, things weren't going at all well with the Israelites. They didn't expect Moses to be gone this long. Maybe they thought he could just say, "Well, Lord, this is taking quite a while, and it's getting late. I have to get back to my people."

It doesn't work that way.

The people really got restless, and finally they rebelled.

And when the people saw that Moses delayed to come down out of the mount, the people gathered themselves together unto Aaron, and said unto him, Up, make us gods, which shall go be-fore us; for as for this Moses, the man that brought us up out of the land of Egypt, we wot not what is become of him. (Exodus 32:1)

When God heard about what was going on with the people, He really got angry. He said, *"Moses, get down there! I'm disgusted with those people!"*

And in His righteous indignation, God was revealing Himself as **Jehovah**. The Lord's personality is that of pure righteousness and holiness. Consider Leviticus 19:2, which says, *"Ye shall be holy: for I the Lord your God am holy."* Translated, this actually means, *"I Jehovah your Elohim am holy."* It is Jehovah Who must pronounce the judgment which condemns sin...and He was really ready to pronounce judgment against the children of Israel for worshipping the gods of Egypt!

God said, *"Moses, you go tell your people that you brought out of Egypt that I will wipe them out! We'll start over again, and I'll make you into a great nation."*

Wait a minute! Are those really Moses' people? In Exodus 3:7, Jehovah had told Moses, *"I have sure seen the affliction of my people."*

10 Now therefore let me alone, that my wrath may wax hot against them, and that I may consume them: and I will make of thee a great nation.

11 And Moses besought the LORD his God, and said, LORD, why doth thy wrath wax hot against thy people which thou has brought forth out of the land of Egypt with great power, and with a mighty hand? (Exodus 32:10-11)

31

Moses had been walking with Jehovah for perhaps a year. He said, "God, **You're** the One Who brought these people forth as their Elohim of power! And they're not my people--they're Yours!"

No one would talk to the Lord like that unless they knew Him really well. Moses was actually arguing with God, Who had already said, *"That's My decision. Now leave me alone!"*

Then Moses said something really interesting.

Wherefore should the Egyptians speak, and say, For mischief did he bring them out, to slay them in the mountains, and to consume them from the face of the earth? Turn from thy fierce wrath, and repent of this evil against thy people. (Exodus 32:12)

What an appeal! I can just see Moses telling Jehovah, "If You kill those people, You are really going to hurt Your reputation, God. The Egyptians are going to say, Look at that God! He's not so hot. He brought those people out into the desert and got mad at them, just like he did at us, and wiped them out!

God, if You wipe them out, Your reputation will be hurt."

Moses was appealing to the Revealing One. But he wasn't quite finished.

Remember Abraham, Isaac, and Israel, thy servants, to whom thou swarest by thine own self, and saidst unto them, I will multiply your seed as the stars of heaven, and all this land that I have spoken of will I give unto your seed, and they shall inherit it for ever. (Exodus

32:13)

Moses prayed God's Word. "God, what about Your promise to Abraham, Isaac, and Jacob? You said You'd make of their seed a great nation--You won't be honoring Your Word."

And what do you think Jehovah did?

And the LORD repented of the evil which he thought to do unto his people. (Exodus 32:14)

Jehovah took the people back as His Own.

Why?

Because Moses prayed the Word; and God says that He magnifies His Word above His name.

Moses went down the mountain with the tablets containing God's commandments. And when he neared the bottom, he discovered why the Lord had been so angry. There was noise, commotion, people dancing...and there sat a golden calf being worshipped.

Moses got angry! He was furious at their sin, probably from spending so much time with Jehovah God, Who loves sinners, but hates sin.

Then Moses stood in the gate of the camp, and said, who is on the Lord's side? let him come unto me. And all the sons of Levi gathered themselves together unto him. (Exodus 32:26)

All of Moses' immediate family from the tribe of Levi came and stood with Moses.

27 And he said unto them, Thus saith the LORD God of Israel, Put every man his sword by his side, and go in and out from gate to gate throughout the camp, and slay every man his brother, and every man his companion, and every man his neighbour.

28 And the children of Levi did according to the word of Moses: and there fell of the people that day about three thousand men. (Exodus 32:27-28)

Moses' successful intercession with God to accept the people didn't mean everything was a bed of roses again. Sin is still sin. Moses gave **all** of the people an opportunity to repent. He argued with God for the people. Then Moses went to the people and told them to stop sinning.

Those who hardened their hearts were put to death. You might think, "Well, they had it tough. No one gets put to death for sinning anymore."

Oh no? Romans 8:6 says, *"to be carnally minded is death; but to be spiritually minded is life and peace."*

Moses gave all of the people a chance to choose life, but only the sons of Levi made the right decision.

After the unrighteous died in battle, Moses went before Jehovah again, and took a priestly stand.

31 And Moses returned to the LORD, and said, Oh, this people have sinned a great sin, and have made them gods of gold.

32 Yet now, if thou wilt forgive their sin--; and if not, blot me, I pray thee, out of thy book which thou has written. (Exodus 32:31-32)

Do you want others to win, or do you just want to win, yourself? If you really want to have a heart that flows with God's will, have a heart like Moses. He had favor with

God, but he used that favor to save his nation. Moses entered into his calling as a priest, and in doing so, he entered into the personality of Jehovah Himself.

33 And the Lord said unto Moses, Whosoever hath sinned against me, him will I blot out of my book.

34 Therefore now go, lead the people unto the place of which I have spoken unto thee: behold, mine Angel shall go before thee: nevertheless in the day when I visit I will visit their sin upon them.

35 And the LORD plagued the people, because they made the calf, which Aaron made. (Exodus 32:33-35)

God still dealt with the people for their sin. Some people will say, "I've repented, so everything is all right."

That is "greasy grace and sloppy agape." There is still a law which began in the very beginning of Genesis, and it is the law of sowing and reaping. Some Christians want to make up their own rules as they go--but they cannot bend that law!

1 And the LORD said unto Moses, Depart, and go up hence, thou and the people which thou hast brought up out of the land of Egypt, unto the land which I sware unto Abraham, to Isaac, and to Jacob, saying, Unto thy seed will I give it:

2 And I will send an angel before thee...

3 ...for I will not go up in the midst of thee; for thou art a stiffnecked people: lest I consume thee in the way. (Exodus 33:1-3)

God told these people, *"I'll send an angel before you to bring you into the Promised Land--but I'm not going, because I cannot stand your rebellion."*

Then the people took off all of their heathen ornaments and stood in the doorways of their tents. Moses went to the tabernacle and entered his priestly role again, to commune with God.

When he got there, the cloud descended upon the tabernacle--and the children of Israel must have thought, "what a relief!"

10 And all the people saw the cloudy pillar stand at the tabernacle door: and all the people rose up and worshipped, every man in his tent door.

11 And the LORD spake unto Moses face to face, as a man speaketh unto his friend. And he turned again into the camp: but his servant Joshua, the son of nun, a young man, departed not out of the tabernacle.

12 And Moses said unto the LORD, See, thou sayest unto me, Bring up this people: and thou has not let me know whom thou wilt send with me. Yet thou hast said, I know thee by name, and thou has also found grace in my sight. (Exodus 33:10-12)

Moses was after God again! He was saying, "God, You haven't said which angel is going to take us into the Promised Land. Remember, God, You called me by name, and gave me grace and favor in Your sight--and if you won't go with us and consider this nation as Your people, we're not going at all!"

Moses could have said, "I've had it with that crowd, and their murmuring!" But he didn't.

How could he talk with God in this way? Because he knew God as **Jehovah**! Moses had an intimate relationship with his Lord.

And what did God say to him?

14 And he said, My presence shall go with thee, and I will give thee rest.

15 And he said unto him, If thy presence go not with me, carry us not up hence. (Exodus 33:14-15)

God went with them. The presence of the Lord was promised by God, and His presence finally brought the people into rest.

But Moses wasn't finished with God. He said, "Lord, I beseech You, show me Your glory."

Moses was a spiritual opportunist, and God liked that quality. God doesn't have pets. Some Christians get more because they stick with it and ask for more! God didn't turn Moses down when he became bold. God said this to Moses.

19 And he said, I will make all my goodness pass before thee, and I will proclaim the name of the LORD before thee; and will be gracious to whom I will be gracious, and will shew mercy on whom I will shew mercy.

20 And he said, Thou canst not see my face: for there shall no man see me, and live.

21 And the LORD said, Behold, there is a place by me, and thou shalt stand upon a rock:

22 And it shall come to pass, while my glory passeth by, that I will put thee in a clift of the rock, and will cover thee with my hand while I pass by:

23 And I will take away mine hand, and thou shalt see my back parts: but my face shall not be seen. (Exodus 33:19-23)

Moses got what he asked for, didn't he?

Why?

Because he was saying, "I want to see Your glory--I desire an even closer relationship with You, Jehovah!"

God has wonderful things in store for those who desire the closeness with Him that Moses had. When I read this, I want to weep, because I really see what the Lord has done for you and me: He has called us to enter our priesthood.

Jehovah did not call us to condemn us--He called us to be reconciled with Him. He called us to reconcile the world to Him, and to make the world winners! Jehovah has called us to go before God in prayer and intercession: "God, have mercy upon them! God, save them!"

What about our priestly calling toward the world? "Get saved! Get right with God, and get the sin out of your life!"

Why?

Because we want people to win. We want them to have life, and have it more abundantly.

38

When you take on the priestly calling of Jehovah (The Lord Who lives in you), He will reveal Himself through you to others.

Jehovah is a beautiful name--the Ever-Revealing One. Zechariah prophesied, saying, In the day of redemption, we shall see **Jehovah.** He prophesied to the nation of Israel, saying, "You are going to look on Him Whom you have pierced."

Who was he talking about?

Jesus!

If you study Jehovah from one end of the Bible to the other, you will find that He is the Lord Jesus Christ: Jehovah, revealed to you!

Jehovah - If you need a special revelation of who God is, read through these scriptures which show Him as LORD. Let Him, the personal, Ever-Revealing One in your life, fill you with the revelation of His redeeming mercy.

But the mercy of the LORD is from everlasting to everlasting upon them that fear him, and his righteousness unto children's children. (Psalm 103:17)

Tell ye, and bring them near; yea, let them take counsel together: who hath declared this from ancient time? who hath told it from that time? have not I the LORD? and there is no God else beside me; a just God and a Saviour; there is none beside me. (Isaiah 45:21)

And I will bring the third part through the fire, and will refine them as silver is refined, and will try them as gold is tried: they shall call on my name, and I will hear them: I will say, It is my people: and they shall say, The LORD is my God. (Zechariah 13:9)

7 The fear of the LORD is the beginning of knowledge: but fools despise wisdom and instruction.

8 My son, hear the instruction of thy father, and forsake not the law of thy mother:

9 For they shall be an ornament of grace unto thy head, and chains about thy neck. (Proverbs 1:7-9)

1 O LORD, thou hast searched me, and known me.

2Thou knowest my downsitting and mine uprising, thou understandest my thought afar off.

3 Thou compassest my path and my lying down, and art acquainted with all my ways.

4 For there is not a word in my tongue, but, lo, O LORD, thou knowest it altogether.

5 Thou hast beset me behind and before, and laid thine hand upon me. (Psalm 139:1-5)

Chapter 3

EL SHADDAI

When you first studied the name Elohim, you discovered that **El** displays God's qualities of power and might. **El shaddai** is also a compound name, which first appears in Genesis 17.

1 And when Abram was ninety years old and nine, the LORD appeared to Abram, and said unto him, I am the Almighty God; walk before me, and be thou perfect.

2 And I will make my covenant between me and thee, and will multiply thee exceedingly. (Genesis 17:1-2)

Does "God Almighty" mean the same as "the God of might and power?" No, it does not.

The name **El Shaddai** bears a different meaning entirely. Basically, this name is derived from the word "field," as the fields produce abundance. It is also trans-

43

lated as "breast," or the "many breasted One," which signifies nourishment and productiveness. In this sense, God is shown as the One Who is more than enough--He Who is all sufficient! When you see the name El Shaddai, God is saying, "I am more than enough to meet your needs in each situation."

Throughout Abraham's life, God promised to bless and multiply him. And the Bible says that Abraham's blessings are also ours. As El Shaddai, God came to Abraham in the context of total impossibility. He came saying, "I'll give you seed as the dust of the earth," when Abraham was 99 years old. And if that's not "impossible" enough, his wife was 89 years old. God shows His all-sufficiency by turning nature around and providing a miracle that is contrary to natural events. Although God Himself set the course of nature in motion, He is more than capable of superceding all natural events! That's what happened when He caused Abraham and Sarah to have a child.

Abraham's son was named Isaac, and Isaac also knew God as El Shaddai. When Isaac's own son Jacob left home to find a wife, Isaac spoke to him.

1 And Isaac called Jacob, and blessed him, and charged him, and said unto him, Thou shalt not take a wife of the daughters of Canaan.

2 Arise, go to Padan-aram, to the house of Bethuel thy mother's father; and take thee a wife from thence of the daughters of Laban thy mother's brother.

3 And God Almighty bless thee, and make thee fruitful, and multiply thee, that thou mayest be a multitude of people. (Genesis 28:1-3)

44

Isaac was saying, "Jacob, may El Shaddai, the God Who is all- sufficient, bless you and multiply you! He will work contrary to nature to overcome any difficult circumstances."

Jacob left home with his father's blessings and the birthright--but with nothing in his hand. In fact, he left behind an irate brother, whom he had cheated out of the birthright. The brother's name was Esau, and he was more than ready to kill Jacob. Jacob had been a "mother's boy," and he was entering a totally strange situation that didn't look prosperous at all!

On the way to Padan-aram, Jacob slept and dreamed of a ladder on which angels ascended and descended. God spoke to him. God said, "I'm giving this land to you and your seed, and I am going to protect you."

Greatly encouraged, Jacob continued on his way. When he arrived, he fell in love with a beautiful girl named Rachel. But Rachel's father Laban didn't possess many beautiful qualities; he was tricky and mean. He told Jacob that he could work seven years to pay for Rachel-- but he gave Jacob Leah, Rachel's older sister, instead. Then Jacob had to work another seven years in order to have Rachel as his wife, too. To look at the situation, Jacob didn't seem very blessed.

To top all of this off, Laban changed Jacob's wages ten times, and he kept stealing Jacob's things. Jacob was in a horrible predicament. Finally, God spoke to him and said, *"I want you to return to the Promised Land."*

Jacob may have thought, "Well, I'll go back poor, but anything is better than living with Laban."

But the God Who is more than enough intended to prosper him.

Some people want everything right away: instant coffee, instant tea, instant answer to prayer. But there's more to it than instant everything. You have to hold fast to your confidence, in order to obtain rewards. You have to be patient and know that God is never late. Sometimes He's just in time, but He is never late. Last minute or not, hold fast to Him the way Jacob did, and you won't miss the recompense of your reward.

God told Jacob, *"I will bless and prosper you, if you will follow these instructions:*

When the cattle are taking water, where they usually mate, place speckled, spotted, and striped stakes in the ground; let them watch the stakes, and you keep your eyes on them, too. Then, when they conceive, they will have speckled, spotted, and striped animals. Those animals will be yours."

Jacob told Laban, "For my hire, I want to take with me all of the speckled, spotted, and striped animals that are born, when I leave."

Laban thought, "Great! There are hardly ever any of those." He told Jacob, "That's just fine."

He really regretted it later, because all of the babies born that year were spotty, speckled, and striped!

Jacob and his animals kept seeing those stakes. God set forth a **vision** to bring His Word to pass, and Jacob left as a very wealthy man.

Why?

Because the all-sufficient El Shaddai was in control. El Shaddai took hold of the natural things and turned them around into supernatural miracles. Jacob knew El Shad-

dai, as did his father, Isaac, and his grandfather, Abraham.
Genesis 35 tells of a third vision Jacob had.

*9 And God appeared unto Jacob again, when
he came out of Padan-aram, and blessed him.*

*10 And God said unto him, Thy name is Jacob:
thy name shall not be called any more Jacob,
but Israel shall be thy name: and he called his
name Israel.*

*11 And God said unto him, I am God Almighty:
be fruitful and multiply; a nation and a com-
pany of nations shall be of thee, and kings shall
come out of thy loins.* (Genesis 35:9-11)

Jacob had lived in the midst of strange circumstances
and strange people, but God said, *"Your situation
doesn't matter! I am what matters. Let Me turn your
circumstances around and bless you!"*

God brought Jacob out from Laban's household as a
wealthy man, reconciled him with his once-angry brother
Esau, and gave him many children. Jacob lived as a
wealthy, blessed man of a ripe, old age, because he knew
El Shaddai.

"Almighty" always relates to blessings and multipli-
cation. Because that name speaks of **more** than enough,
it speaks of abundances. When Jesus said, *"I came to give
you life, and give it to you more abundantly"*, He was
speaking of El Shaddai, Who supplies abundances of nourishment for body, soul, and spirit.

Moses also knew El Shaddai. God spoke to him this
way in Exodus 6.

*And I appeared unto Abraham, unto Isaac,
and unto Jacob, by the name of God Almighty,*

47

but by my name JEHOVAH was I not known to them. (Exodus 6:3)

God was saying, *"I appeared to them as the God Who is more than enough, and I'm speaking to you, too."*

Then Moses wrote this in Psalm 91.

He that dwelleth in the secret place of the most High shall abide under the shadow of the Almighty. (Psalm 91:1)

Then Moses extols the power of God, which delivered them from the plagues that were upon Egypt. In this verse, the word "dwelleth" actually means "to stake your claim." Imagine this: *He that stakes his claim in the secret place of the most High shall abide under the shadow of the almighty.* Moses said, "I'm staking my claim under the shadow of God Who is more than enough. That's where I want to live."

I want to live there, too!

When Moses staked that claim, he really saw results! He was saying, "My God is more than enough to feed two million people. My God is all-sufficient. And even though we're in the wilderness, these two million people will have water. No matter how tough my circumstances may appear, I'm counting on El Shaddai to bring us through!"

And He always did bring them through. That is why Hebrews 11 says that Moses forsook the pleasures of living in the Pharaoh's house, and sojourned in the wilderness with the children of Israel. He stretched his faith out there and said, "I don't need the comforts of Pharaoh's house--my Almighty God has all that I need!"

Throughout his walk with the Lord, Moses kept on seeing the miraculous hand of God overcome nature itself. For forty years, those people had no grocery bill, no water bill, no heating or air conditioning bills, and they never had to buy new shoes or garments.

That is just tremendous--and if God could do it back then for two million people, don't you think He will take care of you now? Stake your claim under the shadow of El Shaddai. He's more than enough--more than you will ever need! Take advantage of what Moses knew; that's why it's there.

Do you want to dwell in the secret place of the Most High? Do you want to abide under the shadow of the Almighty?

I will say of the LORD, He is my refuge and my fortress: my God; in him will I trust. (Psalm 91:2)

Stake your claim with your mouth. Moses did that, and you should, too. Begin saying what you need God to be in your situation: "He's more than enough to heal me. He's more than enough to meet my financial needs; He's more than enough to get my children to repent; He's more than enough to put my marriage back together."

Live under the shadow of the knowledge of a God Who is more than enough. He will turn the natural things around so that you will come through completely whole, and completely blessed!

Did you ever hear of claim jumpers? In Colorado, there are people who stake a claim on land that belongs to someone else. Sometimes they even remove another person's stakes and put theirs up instead.

The devil is a claim jumper, and he'll try to steal what you have claimed. But the Bible says He Who promised is

49

faithful, and you have to push the devil right back off your claim! If you move out and don't hang onto your claim, you'll miss it. If you have already moved out, repent and get back in there! Put your trust in the All Sufficient One.

Joseph is another man who knew El Shaddai. He was Jacob's son, and Jacob prophesied something wonderful over him.

22 Joseph is a fruitful bough, even a fruitful bough by a well; whose branches run over the wall:

23 The archers have sorely grieved him, and shot at him, and hated him:

24 But his bow abode in strength, and the arms of his hands were made strong by the hands of the mighty God of Jacob; (from thence is the shepherd, the stone of Israel:)

25 Even by the God of thy father, who shall help thee; and by the Almighty, who shall bless thee with blessings of heaven above, blessings of the deep that lieth under, blessings of the breasts, and of the womb:

26 The blessings of thy father have prevailed above the blessings of my progenitors unto the utmost bound of the everlasting hills: they shall be on the head of Joseph, and on the crown of the head of him that was separate from his brethren. (Genesis 49:22-26)

Jacob was saying, "Joseph, El Shaddai will bless you abundantly and powerfully with all kinds of prosperity. You will be prospered in every direction that you take, because He is the God of abundances."

Fathers passed the blessings of Almighty God on to their children, because God's promises were to their seed's seed. Notice that Jacob didn't just assume that, because God had said it, his seed would be blessed. He agreed with God and spoke it out loud.

Did it come to pass?

Yes.

Jacob shared one of his visions with Joseph, in Genesis 48.

3And Jacob said unto Joseph, God Almighty appeared unto me at Luz in the land of Canaan, and blessed me,

4 And said unto me, Behold, I will make thee fruitful, and multiply thee, and I will make of thee a multitude of people; and will give this land to thy seed after thee for an everlasting possession. (Genesis 48:3-4)

How could Jacob make all of those bold statements?

Because he knew El Shaddai, and he had his eyes under the shadow of God Who is more than enough.

The Bible says that Abraham's blessings rest upon us. And those blessings are from El Shaddai. That's Jesus saying to you, *"I came to give you life in abundance!"* He never said He came to just squeeze you down into a nub, and to get you into heaven by the skin of your teeth.

No. He has an abundance of God's blessings that are just for you. You need to camp with your mouth under God's shadow, and allow Him to be **more** than enough.

In the book of Numbers, just before the Israelites went forth to take the land of promise, something happened that really ruined it for them. The men went into the land and looked around to see what they would be claiming. When they came back, they said, "The land is beautiful, but there are giants in there. We'll never take the land." Those men brought back an evil report--it was a report that did not agree with the Word of God!

What happened?

God said, "Because you would not let me be **El Shaddai--more than enough to put you over**--you're not going in! Only your children will go in."

Moses' sermons are in the book of Deuteronomy, and his three major sermons are there. He was preaching God's Word to the young men who were supposed to enter and take the Promised Land.

Why?

It's the Word of God that gives people enough faith to take that land!

Faith cometh by hearing, and hearing by the Word of God. He knew, in order to take the promised land, they would have to be mighty men of faith.

When they finally took the land, it was by faith. By that time, Moses had died, and they had to capture a city called Jericho. God gave them a unique battle plan. He told the men to march around the city daily for six days, and seven times on the seventh day.

After they marched around it the last time, He had them shout, and the walls came crashing down! Where did the faith come from? From the preaching of Moses, who told them about God Almighty-**El Shaddai.** He had said, "Place your trust in El Shaddai. He will turn natural circumstances around and give you supernatural miracles!''

El Shaddai--He is the **mighty One** Who can overrule natural events. The book of Numbers tells a story about a man named Balaam, who found out about God's overruling power. Balaam was a man of God, but he had a bad background--he had once been a wizard.

Balaam used to prophesy evil, and put curses on people, just like his father, but then he got turned around, and turned on to God.

During Balaam's life, there was trouble between the Israelites and the people of Moab. The Moabite king was really afraid of the Israelites, because he thought they might start a battle. God had warned the children of Israel to leave the Moabites alone, but this king was still fearful.

Finally, he thought, "If we can put a curse on them, they'll never defeat us in battle.''

That king didn't realize what he was dealing with! It was foolish to him to think that he could defeat the Israelites through occult power.

The king sent for Balaam, and said, "Curse those Israelites, and I'll pay you a lot of money.''

He didn't know that Balaam had become a man of God. Balaam went to the Lord and asked, "What should I do?''

The Lord said, "Don't you dare curse my people! You know better than that, because no one can curse what I have blessed!

That was God's direction to Balaam. After Balaam refused, the Moabites offered him more money.

The devil came to tempt Jesus three times--he'll **always** come back, and you need to make up your mind to stand against his tactics!

Balaam could have stood against those men with the Word of God, but he didn't. Instead, his old nature began to rise up. He was tempted.

He did go before the Lord again, but God had already told him no! Now the Lord said, "Balaam, don't you do anything until they call for you in the morning."

The more Balaam considered that money, the further God's Word slipped from his mind. Instead of heeding God's advice, Balaam thought, "I'm not going to wait around until morning!" And he left on his way to accept the king of Moab's offer.

But look what happened! His donkey crushed his foot on the way, and he even saw an angel. God was really trying to change Balaam's mind about cursing the Israelites. But He will never force anyone to do anything.

God's directive will is in His Word. You can break it and go around it if you desire to, and he won't kill you. But when you're outside of God's will, you're in Satan's territory. And that's exactly where Balaam was treading.

When he got to Moab, the king brought him to a mountaintop and said, "There are the Israelites that I want you to curse." So Balaam started calling for enchantments, trying to bring up demonic spirits, but they wouldn't come.

Instead, you'll be amazed at what happened.

He hath said, which heard the words of God, which saw the vision of the Almighty, falling into a trance, but having his eyes open. (Numbers 24:4)

God put a vision on Balaam. **El Shaddai stepped in** and gave Balaam a supernatural vision which opened his spiritual eyes. There was the Moabite king, waiting to hear Balaam curse the Israelites. This is what Balaam said:

5 How goodly are thy tents, O Jacob, and thy tabernacles, O Israel!

6 As the valleys are they spread forth, as gardens by the river's side, as the trees of lign aloes which the LORD hath planted, and as cedar trees beside the waters. (Numbers 24:5-6)

Balaam just went on and on with wonderful words like that. He even prophesied Jacob's star which led the wise men to Jesus! He prophesied that "God is not a man that He should lie."

What made Balaam say all of those good things? **God's overruling will!** When Balaam tried to bring forth seducing spirits, God just gave him a vision, and all Balaam could speak was the wonderful Word of God!

How could God do this? **He is El Shaddai, the God Who is more than enough!** He is so wonderful that someone tried to curse His people, and He turned that curse in to a **blessing!**

Balak tried three times, on three different mountains, to get Balaam to curse the Israelites, and all Balaam could do was prophesy good things over them.

Finally, Balak said, "You're not doing it at all!"

El Shaddai will work contrary to every natural circumstance, so that **He can be the One Who is All Sufficient!**

Job also knew El Shaddai. The name El Shaddai is used 48 times in the Bible, and 30 of those times are in the book of Job! Job doesn't seem like a book where God would show Himself as more than enough, but **El Shaddai** can.work around total disaster!

When there seemed to be no way out for Job, Almighty God came on the scene and did some of His greatest miracles.

Job lost everything! He lost his children, health, possessions and money. It really looked like he was "down the tubes." In fact, at one point he really would have seemed to be better off dead.

There was Job, lonely, poor, wretched and miserable, when along came a "friend" named Eliphaz who said, "Job! You must have really done something wrong! What did you do to deserve this punishment from God?"

Job had enough trouble without Eliphaz adding to his problems. **BUT**...throughout the book of Job, he kept saying, **"God is more than enough."** He staked his claim under the shadow of Almighty God.

Let us hold fast the profession of our faith without wavering. (Hebrews 10:23)

That is exactly what Job did! Galatians 6:9 says that you will reap in due season--**if** you don't faint!

Job almost fainted--but he had staked a claim, and although he was bent, he didn't break! At the end of the book, God came on the scene and gave Job a double portion of the blessings he had before.

James 5:11 says that you should consider the **end** of Job. I've heard lots of people spend quite a bit of time considering the beginning of Job, but that's not what God's Word emphasized! God is saying, "Hang in there!

Let Me bless you!"

Job ended up with ten more children. He lived about seventy more years. He was tremendously wealthy. His latter years were far more blessed than his former years. But he had to hang on for nine months--and he did it.

How? **He knew El Shaddai.** I can hear Job saying, **"He's more than enough! My God is more than enough!"** He didn't faint, and he reaped his reward.

In the book of Ruth, there is a rather sad story about a woman named Naomi. She moved with her family from Bethlehem into Moab, which was a cursed place.

She shouldn't have moved there, but there was a famine in Bethlehem. She didn't know that God was All Sufficient to feed her family, so they moved.

When she was in Moab, her father and her husband died. Her two sons had disobeyed God by marrying Moabite women, and then they died, too. Naomi was out of God's will. She had blown it. She got out of God's territory and lost all that she had. Was there hope for her?

Have you ever wondered, "Is there hope for me?" Yes, there was hope for her, and there **is** hope for you! If you've blown it, repent and get out of the mess! **El Shaddai can turn it around to your favor.**

Naomi was a defeated woman when she left Moab to return to Bethlehem. But then one of her daughters-in-law ran to meet her. The girl, whose name was Ruth, said, "Your God will be my God! Your land will be my land! I won't leave you, Naomi. I'll live where you live!"

What a comfort. Together, the two women returned to Bethlehem, and when someone saw Naomi, they said,

"Wow! Is that Naomi? She looks terrible--She's so aged looking!" And Naomi's reply was, "Do not call me Naomi. Call me Mara, for the Almighty hath dealt bitterly with me."

I used to think, "What a murmurer!" But then I realized that she was calling God **El Shaddai.** "Yes," she was saying, "I have been in a bitter, ugly situation. But Almighty God, the One Who is more that enough in a bitter situation, can turn it around and change it!" Naomi used the name **Almighty** several times.

What happened? Naomi, whose own children had died, found a daughter in Ruth. She advised Ruth, who married a man named Boaz from the household of Naomi's late husband. And those grandchildren took on Naomi's name!

It may have seemed impossible for Naomi to have a grandchild, but she got to hold that first baby boy, Obed, in her arms!

And best of all, Obed--her grandchild in name--had a son named Jesse. Jesse had a son named David. David was in the lineage of Jesus Christ! A woman who had lost it all was wonderfully blessed because she knew **El Shaddai,** and spoke of Him with her mouth.

Revelation 16:7 and 14 speak about **El Shaddai.** But when I read thoses verses, they didn't seem to fit with the others.

7 And I heard another out of the altar say,
Even so, Lord God Almighty, true and right-
eous are thy judgments. (Revelation 16:7)

This verse continues, and speaks of the outpouring of the fourth vial-judgement. The **Almighty, the God**

Who is more than enough, will pour out more than enough judgement on this world.

14 For they are the spirits of devils, working miracles, which go forth unto the kings of the earth and of the whole world, to gather them to the battle of that great day of God Almighty. (Revelation 16:14)

The **Almighty God** Who is more than enough will pour out more than enough wrath in the end time battle.

And out of his mouth goeth a sharp sword, that with it he should smite the nations: and he shall rule them with a rod of iron: and he treadeth the winepress of the fierceness and wrath of Almighty God. (Revelation 19:15)

I would rather have the blessing of the Almighty than to have His wrath! Whatever God does, He does in abundance. You have to make a choice of which you would rather have--abundance of blessing or wrath.

You can't stand in the middle and choose neither. It's blessings and abundances, or it's wrath. The day is coming when God is going to judge the earth. Choose His abundance. **Choose for Him to be All-Sufficient in every one of your situations. El Shaddai**--what a name to camp under! Have you staked your claim?

EL Shaddai - El Shaddai wants to be More Than Enough to you. **Speak of Him. Get to know Him, and trust Him as the ALL SUFFICIENT ONE.** Here are some scriptures which portray God as El Shaddai.

19 And to know the love of Christ, which passeth knowledge, that ye might be filled with all the fulness of God.

20 Now unto him that is able to do exceeding abundantly above all that we ask or think, according to the power that worketh in us,

21 Unto him be glory in the church by Christ Jesus throughout all ages, world without end. Amen. (Ephesians 3:19-21)

...Behold, I will make thee fruitful, and multiply thee, and I will make of thee a multitude of people; and will give this land to thy seed after thee for an everlasting possession. (Genesis 48:4)

2 Every branch in me that beareth not fruit he taketh away: and every branch that beareth fruit, he purgeth it, that it may bring forth more fruit.

16 Ye have not chosen me, but I have chosen you, and ordained you, that ye should go and bring forth fruit, and that your fruit should remain: that whatsoever ye shall ask of the Father in my name, he may give it you. (John 15:2,16)

Chapter 4

ADONAI

The names you have studied so far--Elohim, Jehovah, and El Shaddai--have all related to the **person** of God. Elohim has expressed the might and power of God. Jehovah has expressed the holiness and righteousness of God as our Redeemer. And you have seen Him as a wonderful God of blessings and all-sufficiency as El Shaddai.

Translated in your King James Bible as "Lord," **Adonai** is a somewhat different name for God, in that it reflects our responsibility as His servants.

The Lord wants to say something special to you through this name. Knowing Him as Adonai will help you in making a deeper commitment to Him. I get excited about teaching who Adonai is, and you will be excited about putting this truth to use in your life.

Adonai is used over 300 times in the Old Testament alone, and it literally means "Master," "Owner," or

"Lord." This is a name which signifies **ownership**, and our own responsibilities, coming from being owned by God.

There is an interesting facet of Adonai that is found only in another of God's names--Elohim. Adonai can be translated as being both **plural** and **possessive**, so it confirms the fact of a triune Godhead: Father, Son, and Holy Spirit. When used to describe men, the singular word "adon" is used. But when describing God, the word becomes **Adonai**. It is so exciting to see God, Jesus, and the Holy Spirit involved in this wonderful name. And their involvement is confirmed in Psalm 110.

The LORD said unto my Lord, Sit thou at my right hand, until I make thine enemies thy footstool. (Psalm 110:1)

Plurality in the name Adonai is further confirmed in this scripture from the New Testament.

Therefore let all the house of Israel know assuredly, that God hath made that same Jesus, whom ye have crucified, both Lord and Christ. (Acts 2:36)

God, as our Adonai, is in the position of being the Master, and we His purchased possession. Exodus 21 offers a picture of this relationship.

1 Now these are the judgments which thou shalt set before them.

2 If thou buy an Hebrew servant, six years he shall serve: and in the seventh he shall go out free for nothing.

3 If he came in by himself, he shall go out by himself: if he were married, then his wife shall go out with him.

4 If his master have given him a wife, and she have born him sons or daughters; the wife and her children shall be her master's, and he shall go out by himself.

5 And if the servant shall plainly say, I love my master, my wife, and my children; I will not go out free:

6 Then his master shall bring him unto the judges; he shall also bring him to the door, or unto the door post; and his master shall bore his ear through with an aul; and he shall serve him for ever. (Exodus 21:1-6)

The Israelites allowed slavery on a limited basis. If a man were so poor that he could not support himself financially, and was in danger of poverty and starvation, he could approach another Israelite and say, "Could I be your slave for six years?"

As a slave, this man was responsible to obey every order; and his master would provide his food, lodging, direction, and protection for those six years. Slaves were subject to all of the master's desires.

After serving a master for six years, in the seventh year, slaves were allowed to go free. At the time of departure, masters were responsible to supply their former slaves with a certain amount of material wealth. If a man had married before enslavement and brought his wife along, she and any of their children would go free. If, however, the master had provided the wife, she and any of her children born into slavery would stay behind, but the man could leave free. Naturally, men who were loving husbands and fathers would certainly not want to leave their wives and children!

Should a slave decide to remain in slavery to his master, they would pierce the servant's ear with an awl, and plug the hole with the master's coat of arms, or a special color.

What did this symbolize?

This was the slave's way of saying, "I am a slave by my own choice. I will never be free, and my master has obtained my total obedience for life. I am a willing slave whose master is totally responsible over me." This person was called a **bondslave**.

Adonai is the God Who totally owns His people. He protects them, provides for them, and directs them. Adonai is the Master Whose servants have chosen to serve Him because they love Him. This is a beautiful illustration of the Father-Son relationship that takes place between God and Jesus. Jesus came to earth by the Father's will, to redeem us. He never sinned, because He was carrying out the responsibility that His Father gave Him.

The Bible says, when Jesus' time of physical death approached, He entered a garden called Gethsemane to pray. The account is in Luke 22.

42 Father, if thou be willing, remove this cup from me: nevertheless not my will, but thine, be done.

43 And there appeared an angel unto him from heaven, strengthening him.

44 And being in an agony he prayed more earnestly: and his sweat was as it were great drops of blood falling down to the ground. (Luke 22:42-44)

The garden of Gethsemane saw a struggle that day. I believe the Father said, *"Son, You don't have to drink of this cup. But it is Your bride (Israel) and many children (the church)."*

By saying, *"Not My will, but Yours be done,"* Jesus was saying, *"I am more than Your servant; I am a **bondslave** to My Father's will. I came here to complete My Father's will, so I am willing to be pierced."*

Adonai--Master, and Lord of lords, displayed through the Father, the Son, and the Holy Spirit.

Jesus' hands and feet were nailed onto a cross. His flesh was cruelly beaten, and His side was pierced with a sword.

Why?

Because He became a bondslave to the Father; One Who said, *"No matter the cost--it's **Your** will, not **Mine.**"*

Jesus gave Himself as a slave:

5 Let this mind be in you, which was also in Christ Jesus:

6 Who, being in the form of God, thought it not robbery to be equal with God:

7 But made himself of no reputation, and took upon him the form of a servant, and was made in the likeness of men. (Philippians 2:5-7)

Jesus, the bondslave to His Father, willingly hung upon a cross. He was willingly pierced, because He loves you. And today He still carries the signs of His bondslavery. In the Old testament, slaves may have had plugs in their ears. But Jesus' enslavement has marked Him beyond that: He has a scar on His side, and in His hands and feet. There are scars upon His back and head. Those marks say one thing: **Bondslave**. Zechariah 12:10 says, *"They shall look upon me whom they have pierced, and they shall mourn for him, as one mourneth for his only son...."*

Those people who pierced Jesus will look upon Him again in the Day of Judgment.

Like Psalms 110:1 and Acts 2:36, this verse from Zechariah also confirms the plurality within the name **Adonai.**

Many people really cringe at the thought of God having complete ownership over them. A lot of people have been conformed to the world's image of thinking; "I have to be my own person," or, "I'm just a free spirit."

You are not a free spirit! You have been purchased for the expensive price of the Lord's own blood. But even better than that, First Corinthians 7:22 says, *"For he that is called in the Lord, being a servant, is the Lord's freeman."*

The only freeing Spirit is the Holy Spirit, Who is in agreement with the Father and Son. It's in becoming a **bondslave to** Adonai that you will be free **in** Him!

...where the Spirit of the Lord is, there is liberty. (2nd Corinthians 3:17)

And unto man he said, Behold, the fear of the Lord, that is wisdom; and to depart from evil is understanding. (Job 28:28)

The fear of the LORD is the beginning of wisdom.... (Proverbs 9:10)

Job was saying, *"Behold, the fear of Adonai--that is wisdom!"* To respect the Lord and give Him total ownership is the wisest thing you will ever do. "Fear" does not mean, in this context, that you are cowering and afraid. "Fear" means respect and reverence of Him as your Master; it denotes willingly making Him the Owner and Master over your life. He wants to totally provide for you, protect and direct you--but you must first use the wisdom that lets Him do that. Make Adonai your Master!

You can receive Jesus as your Savior and still not make Him the Master of your life. In fact, many people receive Him without ever realizing that He wants to be the master over their lives. But Jesus doesn't want us calling the shots.

If you are still at the reins in your life, then you are not entering into the Lord's fullness. Revelation knowledge of God's Word and victory can only come to His children one way: when they put Adonai in the place of **control!**

Genesis 15 tells about some people who decided to make God the Master over their lives.

And Abram said, Lord GOD, what wilt thou give me, seeing I go childless, and the steward of my house is this Eliezer of Damascus? (Genesis 15:2)

In this chapter, God and Abram made a covenant together. God identified Abraham's seed that would number as the stars of heaven, and the dust of the earth. But God did not covenant with Abram until he had said, "Lord God--Adonai Elohim."

Abram was saying, "Yes, You are the God of power and might. You are also my Master."

Have you ever wondered, "I thought I had a covenant with the Lord--why aren't His promises coming to pass in my life?"

I have a question for you: have you made Him your Master?

Moses was smart--he made God his Master. It is recorded in Exodus 4:10.

And Moses said unto the LORD, O my Lord, I am not eloquent, neither heretofore, nor since thou hast spoken unto thy servant: but I am slow of speech, and of a slow tongue. (Exodus 4:10)

Moses said this when he was trying to get out of leading the children of Israel out of Egypt. But he prefaced it by saying, "You're the Master, and I'll do it, because You're my Owner. You're my Protector, and You give me direction for my life."

The book of Judges has some key things for you to read. They explain that God wants to bless His people; He wants to deliver them out of negative situations, but He cannot do it, if they won't let Him be the Master. In the book of Judges, Israel was in a very backslidden condition. They had taken the Promised Land--but they left the Word (the Promises) behind! In Judges, they were involved with idolatry and sin. And then, everything fell apart.

A wicked king named Chushanishathaim came to battle against Israel, and his name really fits. It means "double wickedness." Maybe that's why it's so long.

A man named Othniel was Israel's first judge--in office at the time--and he had a wonderful family tree. His father-in-law was Caleb, who was full of God's Spirit. It was a good thing Caleb was still around when Chushan-rishathaim came against Israel--they could have easily lost the fight. But God gave Caleb a special anointing to fight, and Israel was delivered marvelously.

But what happened as soon as this conflict ended? The Israelites slipped right back into idolatry again. They returned to doing their own thing. And this time they paid the piper. The Midianites were allowed by God to overwhelm them. Fires raged through the crops, destroying huge plots of land. Men, women, children were killed, and their households were plundered. Terror caused many people to desperately dig holes in the ground where they could hide. Others dwelt in caves. Idolatry had once again cost Israel a dear price.

One day, a man named Gideon was about his business when an angel of the Lord appeared to him, saying, "Gideon, you mighty man of valor!"

Gideon may have looked around to see who else the angel was talking to. But he was all alone; the angel **was** talking to him. Full of anxiety, Gideon said this.

Oh my Lord (Master or Owner), if the LORD be with us, why then is all this befallen us? And where be all his miracles which our fathers told us of, saying, Did not the LORD bring us up from Egypt? but now the LORD hath forsaken us, and delivered us into the hands of the Midianites. (Judges 6:13)

Gideon was saying, "If we have such a great Master and Owner, why isn't He protecting us? Why isn't He providing for us? Why isn't He directing us?" Gideon had said the words that needed to be said: **Master. Owner. Adonai.**

Then the angel said this to Gideon.

14 Go in this thy might, and thou shalt save Israel from the hand of the Midianites: have not I sent thee?

15 And he said unto him, Oh my Lord, wherewith shall I save Israel? behold, my family is poor in Manasseh, and I am the least in my father's house. (Judges 6:14-15)

The angel said, "Gideon, you are going to deliver your people."

Gideon may have thought, "I had to complain. See what happens when you open your mouth?"

He had some real excuses, too: "we're poor! I'm a nobody!"

All of that was really untrue, because Gideon's father was once the leading man in his town. Gideon was their key son, who had a real future in Manasseh. But that was before the Midianites had destroyed things. Now Gideon had a poor, fearful self-image.

The angel kept saying, "Gideon, you're a mighty man of valor!" to overcome Gideon's terrible inferiority complex. Perhaps he felt so inferior and cowardly that he actually became that way. But when God is your Master and Owner, He will put you over.

Many people think the word "Master" describes someone who will squeeze them under his thumb. That is not true of God! He wants to lift you up and put you over: "Gideon, you mighty man of valor!"

God looks at you in the light of His Word--not yours! He sees you in the image of Jesus Himself. Adonai, as master, wants you to be very, very victorious, so He speaks positive words: His Word! Adonai wants to protect you and care for you. But if you won't let Him, then He can't. Gideon did the right thing when he said, "Master;" and then the words of deliverance came.

Finally, Gideon said, *"...If now I have found grace in thy sight, then shew me a sign that thou talkest with me."* (Judges 6:17)

The angel was willing. Gideon prepared a sacrifice, and presented it as the angel directed him.

20 And the angel of God said unto him, Take the flesh and the unleavened cakes, and lay them upon this rock, and pour out the broth. And he did so.

21 Then the angel of the LORD put forth the end of the staff that was in his hand, and touched the flesh and the unleavened cakes; and there rose up fire out of the rock, and consumed the flesh and the unleavened cakes.

22 And when Gideon perceived that he was an angel of the LORD, Gideon said, Alas, O Lord GOD! for because I have seen an angel of the LORD face to face. (Judges 6:20-22)

The Master-Owner allowed Gideon to see a miracle, so he would confess and agree that he was indeed a mighty man of valor. Instead, Gideon showed the worst self-image ever. He cried out, "Oh! I've seen the Lord, so I'm going to die!"

Obviously he didn't realize that the Word of God is practical--how could Gideon be a deliverer, if God were to kill him?

If fear overtakes you, be practical with God's Word--and the fear will leave!

23 And the LORD said unto him, Peace be unto thee; fear not: thou shalt not die.

24 Then Gideon built an altar there unto the LORD, and called it Jehovah-shalom: unto this day it is yet in Ophrah of the Abiezrites. (Judges 6:23-24)

Gideon built an altar because God had given him peace. God was still trying to get Gideon to speak and believe that He was the Master of the situation. After this, Gideon became bolder; he pulled down the altar of Baal and built an altar to the Lord.

The idolatrous people got upset when they discovered that their statue of Baal had been pulled down. Then someone said, "I think Gideon pulled it down."

Who told them? I think God did. I think He was a tattle-tale so that Gideon would have to come out of the woodwork. They said, "Gideon pulled this down! We'll kill him for that!"

Gideon's father stepped out. He told them to wait just a minute; he said, *"Will ye plead for Baal?...if he be a god, let him plead for himself, because one hath cast down his altar."* (Judges 6:31)

The people agreed to this, and they told Gideon, "Baal's going to get you!" Of course, Baal couldn't possibly "get him," so Gideon's life was spared.

When harvest time arrived, the Midianites arrived also. They gathered together, covering the valley of Israel by the thousands, and prepared for an attack.

Where was Gideon? Even though God had spoken to him and he had seen a miracle, and even though God had given him peace and spared him, Gideon was still hiding, full of fear.

Then something happened.

But the Spirit of the LORD came upon Gideon, and he blew a trumpet; and Abiezer was gathered after him. (Judges 6:34)

The Hebrew wording for "the Spirit of the LORD came upon Gideon" says that he "was clothed in the Spirit from his head to his toes." Why did God clothe Gideon with His Spirit?

Because he needed it; he was so full of holes!

Then Gideon gathered men together to fight against the Midianites, and God said, *"Whosoever is fearful and afraid, let him return and depart."* At this point, Gideon discovered that he wasn't the only one who had experienced an inferiority complex. Of 32,000 men, 22,000 went home.

Why would God allow most of the people to leave? Because He was about to show Himself as the Master Who protects! When God is your Master and Owner, He will put you over.

God then told Gideon, "Tell everyone to take a drink of water from this lake. And send home everyone who puts their face into the water to drink. Keep only the ones who take their water with their hands."

Why only the men who took the water from their hands? Because their eyes were up from the water--they were watching for the enemy!

Gideon was left with only 300 men. God would **have** to be the Master over this situation!

The 300 men went to battle against the Midianite army, and the Lord gave them an unusual battle plan.

16 And he divided the three hundred men into three companies, and he put a trumpet in every man's hand, with empty pitchers, and lamps within the pitchers.

17 And he said unto them, Look on me, and do likewise: and, behold, when I come to the outside of the camp, it shall be that, as I do, so shall ye do.

18 When I blow with a trumpet, I and all that are with me, then blow ye the trumpets also on every side of all the camp, and say, The sword of the LORD, and of Gideon. (Judges 7:16-18)

The Midianites were defeated! How did that all come to pass? It came to pass because of a man who called God **Adonai--Master!**

Isaiah the prophet was willing to be God's bondslave, and he wrote all 66 chapters of the book of Isaiah. He ministered to four kings, and had the greatest revelation of the Son of God that any prophet received. He saw the redemption of Jesus Christ, and the book that he authored is called the "Gospel of the Old Testament."

Why?

Because he made a total commitment that said, "God, You be my Owner. You call the shots."

74

When Isaiah saw the Lord as Master and Owner, he reacted by saying, *"I am a man of unclean lips."* When he said that, a seraphim placed a white-hot coal upon his lip, and the Lord began speaking about his responsibility.

5 Then said I, Woe is me! for I am undone; because I am a man of unclean lips, and I dwell in the midst of a people of unclean lips: for mine eyes have seen the King, the LORD of hosts.

6 Then flew one of the seraphims unto me, having a live coal in his hand, which he had taken with the tongs from off the altar:

7 And he laid it upon my mouth, and said, Lo, this hath touched thy lips; and thine iniquity is taken away, and thy sin purged.

8 Also I heard the voice of the Lord, saying, Whom shall I send, and who will go for us? Then said I, Here am I; send me. (Isaiah 6:5-8)

Acts 9 tells the story of another young man who called God **Adonai**. In the beginning of his story, he was on the road for Damascus--on his way to persecute and kill the Christians. While traveling, a brilliant light shone upon him, blinding the man's eyes. A voice spoke. *"Saul, Saul, why persecutest thou me?"*

Saul said, "Who are you, **Lord**?"

Immediately, Saul's heart was softened, and the Lord could deal with him.

Why?

Because Saul said, "You are my Master."

According to Job 28:28, acknowledging God as your Master brings forth revelation knowledge of God and His

Word. Calling Him Adonai, Paul received a wonderful revelation.

> *5 And the Lord said, I am Jesus whom thou persecutest: it is hard for thee to kick against the pricks.*
>
> *6 And he trembling and astonished said, Lord, what wilt thou have me to do? And the Lord said unto him, Arise, and go into the city, and it shall be told thee what thou must do. (Acts 9:5-6)*

What happened? Saul made Jesus the Lord of his life--the Master of all that he was. Saul's name was changed to Paul, and he continued getting revelation knowledge--and eventually wrote over one-third of the New Testament!

Why?

Because at the beginning of his spiritual life, Paul did more than take Jesus as his Savior--he took Him as Lord: **Adonai!** You too must make Him Master.

Acts 23 tells about a time when Paul was in a lot of trouble with the Jews. He was teaching, and they were in hot disagreement, so they started planning to kill him. It was then that Paul said, "The real problem is that the Sadducees are mad at the Pharisees because the Pharisees believe in angels, and the resurrection. That's why I'm being called up for the trouble here."

God turned this situation around, for Paul was about to be killed, and then the Pharisees and Sadducees ended up fighting with each other! Maybe it didn't matter who they were fighting with--they just liked a good fight.

*And the night following the Lord stood by him,
and said, Be of good cheer, Paul: for as thou
hast testified of me in Jerusalem, so must thou
bear witness also at Rome.* (Acts 23:11)

How that must have encouraged Paul's heart! His
Master and Owner stood by him. Paul called on the Lord,
because he needed the protection that only his Master
could give.

*For he that is called in the Lord (Master,
Owner), being a servant (bondslave), is the
Lord's freeman: likewise also he that is called,
being free, is Christ's servant.* (2nd Corinthians
7:22)

Commitment is essential in order to have results! If
you want to be totally free, be one hundred percent committed to the Lord as His bondslave. When you place Him
in command and follow His direction, you are free from
worry, fear, or anything devilish! You are **free!**

Nations were affected, and history has been affected
by people who have said, **Adonai! Master!** to the Lord.

You can affect your world by making God your
Adonai! Is He your Savior? Then you must also make Him
the Lord over your life! The two go hand in hand.

Now I want you to pray this prayer of committal out
loud to God:

Dear heavenly Father, I come to You in Jesus'
Name, and call You my **Lord.** I thank You for
giving me Jesus as my Savior, but I now choose
Him as Lord over my Life! Jesus, You take over
and call the shots now! I'm Your bondslave, my
Master. Praise the Lord! Amen.

Adonai - Jesus wants to be much more than Savior to you. He wants to be your Adonai, Master and Owner. Is He the Master over your life? Are you allowing His tender protection to keep you each day? The scriptures offer a beautiful picture of your relationship with Him: the bondservant and Lord.

Behold , as the eyes of servants look unto the hand of their masters, and as the eyes of a maiden unto the hand of her mistress; so our eyes wait upon the Lord our God, until that he have mercy upon us. (Psalm 123:2)

But do thou for me, O God the Lord, for thy name's sake: because thy mercy is good, deliver thou me. (Psalm 109:21)

For ye are bought with a price: therefore glorify God in your body, and in your spirit, which are God's. (1 Corinthians 6:20)

21 Art thou called being a servant? care not for it: but if thou mayest be made free, use it rather.

22 For he that is called in the Lord, being a servant, is the Lord's freeman: likewise also he that is called, being free, is Christ's servant.

23 Ye are bought with a price; be not ye the servants of men.

24 Brethren, let every man, wherein he is called, therein abide with God. (1st Corinthians 7:21-24)

Chapter 5

JEHOVAH JIREH

Before you discover Who Jehovah Jireh is to you, review the qualities of Jehovah's personality: He is the Revealing One, revealing His ways to you. He is eternal and changeless. He is a God of righteousness and holiness Who judges sin. And He is the God Who is full of mercy--our Redeemer!

Jehovah Jireh is the first compound name of Jehovah to appear in the Old Testament, and it beautifully expands the meaning of Jehovah's Name. Genesis twenty-two is the first chapter in the Bible where the name **Jehovah Jireh** appears, after the Lord showed Himself to Abraham on the basis of meeting his needs.

When you discover how this name applies to you, you will know that Jehovah Jireh not only met Abraham's needs, but also desires to meet **YOUR** needs. Remember, Jehovah is the eternal changeless One Who reveals His ways to you.

By calling Himself Jehovah Jireh, He is saying this:

"I do not change--My ways do not change. Therefore, I desire to meet your needs, just as I met the needs of the children of Israel in their exodus from Egypt."

The purpose of learning God's Names is not to give you head knowledge of Who He is. The reason is to increase the closeness of your relationship with Him. You should know Who your God is, for He wants you to know. That is why He revealed Himself through different names.

Store this study inside your Spirit and use the information to personalize the scriptures. Say, "That's Adonai! He's my God and my Father!" Let Him reveal Himself to you in **YOUR** existence, and **YOUR** environment to meet **YOUR** need.

Jehovah Jireh's Name first arose during the life of Abraham, when he faced perhaps the most difficult trial of his faith:

1 And it came to pass after these things, that God did tempt Abraham, and said unto him, Abraham: and he said, Behold, here I am.

2 And he said, Take now thy son, thine only son Isaac, whom thou lovest, and get thee into the land of Moriah; and offer him there for a burnt offering upon one of the mountains which I will tell thee of. (Genesis 22:1-2)

When it says that "God did tempt Abraham," don't get the wrong idea. God was not trying to "see what Abraham was made of." He already knew. He only wanted Abraham to test and **prove** the Word in his own life.

When this incident occurred, Abraham was at least one hundred and twenty years old. He had walked with the Lord for almost fifty years. He was a strong man of God's Word, and **he was growing in the knowledge of God.**

Faith is not a static condition--it wasn't that for Abraham, and it should not be that way for you. God causes people to **move**: from faith to faith, from glory to glory, and from strength to strength. When God spoke to Abraham, He was giving him an opportunity to **MOVE** in his faith.

When you receive answers to prayer and get to see God's Word perform mightily, doesn't that encourage your faith? It does mine. That's God's way of encouraging you to take bigger and bolder steps.

When The Lord asked Abraham to offer Isaac as a sacrifice, He wasn't calling him from out of the blue--they had been walking together for about fifty years. They had a **covenant relationship!** God was saying,

Take now thy son, thine only son Isaac, whom thou lovest, and get thee into the land of Moriah; and offer him there for a burnt offering upon one of the mountains which I will tell the of. (Genesis 22:2)

This was **an offering of consecration!** This was the peak of Abraham's faith. After all, he had waited for Isaac for twenty-five years before he received him--and then had received him through a miracle, at that! How many people do you know who have had a child when they were eighty-nine or ninety-nine years old? But God had promised to provide "seed" for Abraham, and He was

81

faithful who promised.

Finally Abraham had his son, Isaac, and now God was asking him to offer Isaac as a sacrifice. What did Abraham do? He stood tall and didn't stagger at what God was asking. He must have thought,

"If God can give me a son when I'm ninety-nine years old, He'll make sure that His promise is kept. I am going to have seed as the dust of the earth!"

And Abraham rose up early in the morning, and saddled his ass, and took two of his young men with him, and Isaac his son, and clave the wood for the burnt offering, and rose up, and went unto the place of which God had told him.
(Genesis 22:3)

If I had been Abraham, I probably would have slept in that morning. But Abraham did not fall apart over what God was asking.

Why?

Because he wasn't being led by his senses. He was being led by his spirit man.

Abraham had the wonderful quality of a man who **considered God above his circumstances!** He didn't leave out a single preparation that morning. He saddled his animals, and brought along servants to accompany Isaac and himself. He even brought wood for the offering. **He obeyed** the Lord's request to the last detail.

The offering which Abraham was about to make was one of **consecration.** There are five different types of offerings. They are shown in the book of Leviticus. They are:

1. The consecration offering - voluntary
2. The meal offering - voluntary
3. The peace offering - voluntary
4. The trespass offering - mandatory
5. The sin offering - mandatory

Three of these offerings are voluntary, and two of them are mandatory.

Abraham was making a burnt **consecration offering**, which involves **consecrating one's life**. There are times in our lives when we ought to **set aside a special time for fasting and prayer.** We might say,

"God, for the next three nights I will fast dinner and pray for two hours each night."

These are times which are set aside in our lives, specifically for the purpose of seeking God and consecrating ourselves totally to Him. Perhaps you give Him a special time by going witnessing on a door-to-door basis. You aren't required to do these things. You won't be lost if you don't do them. It is a form of **willing commital.**

That's what the offering of Isaac was. Abraham was saying,

"God, I consecrate my son to you. I give what I love the most to You."

The meal offering was also voluntary. It is similar to our tithes that we give today. The people would bring flour or bread, and they would offer it to the Lord as a part of their substance. It was a way of saying, "God, You are my source of blessing. I consecrate my blessings to You."

The peace offering was a voluntary celebration of peace with God. Men often brought family and friends along when they made this offering. Our equivalent today might be our **taking communion together.**

The trespass offering was a mandatory one. It was made when one had trespassed against a person. **Trespasses separate people from God.** Don't allow them to bring separation from Him into your life. Be quick to repent of trespasses against others.

The sin offering was also mandatory. It involved an offering which was made when one sinned against God. Sin must always be repented of. I believe Jesus' cross points this out for this reason: God wants our relationships to be right with Him, and with others.

Offerings weren't ordinarily given during Abraham's time. There are none recorded until the book of Leviticus, except for this instance. But this offering which God asked Abraham to make was a "picture" of the burnt offerings which were to be made in the future.

While Abraham was journeying toward Moriah, which is a mountain range, he did something that is very significant of his faith.

Then on the third day Abraham lifted up his eyes, and saw the place afar off. (Genesis 22:4)

The book of Genesis tells of three separate times when Abraham "lifted up his eyes." Each time, he was doing more than just looking around to see the view. Abraham wasn't looking at what he could see with his natural vision, he was entering a "visionary" faith realm. He was catching a vision of what God wanted him to see.

There are times when God wants us to lift up our eyes and see the spiritual vision of what He is giving us. When God wants to give you something special, you must be very keen spiritually, in order to receive it. That is why consecration is so essential. It keeps you sensitive to the things of the Lord. I believe, when Abraham lifted up his eyes, he was looking at the promises of God, and **considering his circumstances in light of those promises.**

Scanning the mountain range of Moriah, Abraham pinpointed his vision on the mountain to which he was taking his son, Isaac, to be sacrificed. By lifting up his eyes, he was taking his vision off the natural. He was looking to where God wanted him to look, **putting his vision on God's Word.**

What was Abraham's faith vision? Hebrews 11:17-19 tells you what he saw.

17 By faith Abraham, when he was tried, offered up Isaac: and he that had received the promises offered up his only begotten son,

18 Of whom it was said that in Isaac shall thy seed be called:

19 Accounting that God was able to raise him up, even from the dead; from whence also he received him in a figure. (Hebrews 11:17-19)

What is a figure? It is a **faith vision.** When Abraham lifted his eyes and saw Moriah, he saw himself sacrificing Isaac. In his heart, he considered the sacrifice to already be done. And he saw something more than that. Abraham saw the son for whom he'd waited twenty-five years, being raised up out of the ashes by God!

For that reason, he could be faithful to God during this trial.

A lot of people say, "Well, Abraham saw his son being resurrected. That's nothing new, Jesus was resurrected."

Abraham believed in resurrection before anyone else had ever seen or heard of it! No wonder he is called the "father of faith." He did not live according to his senses. He lived directed by the spirit, in the realm of faith visions. Abraham lived according to Proverbs 4:20-22.

20 My son, attend to my words; incline thine ear unto my sayings.

21 Let them not depart from thine eyes; keep them in the midst of thine heart.

22 For they are life unto those that find them, and health to all their flesh. (Proverbs 4:20-22)

The Word that Abraham did not let depart from before his eyes was:

...I will make thy seed to multiply as the stars of heaven. (Genesis 26:4)

And I will make thy seed as the dust of the earth. (Genesis 13:16)

...and make thy seed as the sand of the sea. (Genesis 32:12)

He was saying, "I can't have that, if Isaac doesn't raise from the dead, because God called him my promised seed. God won't neglect His promise--He is faithful Who promised, and I won't let His Word depart from before my eyes!"

I take God's Word literally, and you should too. Practice what it says each day. If you have children in rebellion, and you're hearing and seeing bad things, don't focus on them. You cannot afford to let God's Word depart from before your eyes. **You must hold fast to His Word--your confidence--in order to see your reward.**

Your confidence has great recompense of reward! It has your children. What you are to see is God's Word, saying,

...the seed of the righteous shall be delivered.
(Proverbs 11:21)

And you are the righteousness of God in Christ Jesus. Let the Word of God deliver your children--keep it before you!

And Abraham said unto his young men, Abide ye here with the ass; and I and the lad will go yonder and worship, and come again to you. (Genesis 22:5)

If I had to sacrifice my son, I don't think I'd refer to it as **worship!** Was Abraham's offering of Isaac "worship?" Remember, he had a faith vision!

If you have a faith vision, you must have a faith mouth. How can you see and believe one thing by faith, while you're saying something completely different? You can't. If what you say is not in agreement with what God says, then you need to change what you are saying!

Abraham had the right idea. He was saying words in exact agreement with his faith vision. Abraham's statement became really bold when he said that he and his son would return again to the servants!

Hold fast your confession of faith. If Abraham had griped, "I waited twenty-five years for Isaac, and now

God wants me to kill him," it would have been a pity party. And the only one who will be at your pity party is you! Pity parties don't pay off--only faith parties pay off.

6 And Abraham took the wood of the burnt offering, and laid it upon Isaac his son; and he took the fire in his hand, and a knife; and they went both of them together.

7 And Isaac spake unto Abraham his father, and said, My father: and he said, Here am I, my son. And he said, Behold the fire and the wood: but where is the lamb for the burnt offering?

8 And Abraham said, My son, God will provide himself a lamb for a burnt offering: so they went both of them together. (Genesis 22:6-8)

I think this would have been the hardest part of all. It would have been easy for Abraham to fall apart! Why didn't he say,

"Oh, Isaac, you are the lamb."

He didn't say that because he was holding fast to the profession of his faith, **for God is faithful Who promised.** Abraham's words created a miracle, and so can your words. Again, faith seeing and speaking go hand in hand. Abraham stuck with God's promise, and when he did, something wonderful happened!

9 And they came to the place which God had told him of; and Abraham built an altar there, and laid the wood in order, and bound Isaac his son, and laid him on the altar upon the wood.

10 And Abraham stretched forth his hand, and took the knife to slay his son.

11 And the angel of the LORD called unto him out of heaven, and said, Abraham, Abraham: and he said, Here am I.

12 And he said, Lay not thine hand upon the lad, neither do thou any thing unto him: for now I know that thou fearest God, seeing thou hast not withheld thy son, thine only son from me.

13 And Abraham lifted up his eyes, and looked, and behold behind him a ram caught in a thicket by his horns: and Abraham went and took the ram, and offered him up for a burnt offering in the stead of his son. (Genesis 22:9-13)

Abraham lifted up his eyes again, and this time God let him see a spiritual provision for the natural realm--that is, a physical thing which was provided through spiritual means.

When you pray, believe that you will see God's provision. Let him direct your eyes to the place in His Word that strengthens your belief in Him. The Lord desires to give you hearing ears and seeing eyes that will see His provision for you.

After the ram had been offered up as a burnt offering of consecration, Abraham looked at the place and gave it a name: **JEHOVAH JIREH: the Revealing One Who is more than a Provider.** This name is actually taken from the verb **to see** in the Hebrew.

What does that mean?

It means God has seen ahead and made a provision to fill your need!

There is not one trial nor problem which you may be encountering that God has not already seen. You cannot have anything going on that He hasn't already seen and made provision to take care of.

Why?

Because **He is your Jehovah Jireh,** just as He was Abraham's Jehovah Jireh. He knows **all** things. He already knows what you will encounter in your life, and He has a provision for you to handle it.

If you are in the midst of a trial right now, lift up your eyes! Say,

"God, You saw ahead and knew that I would encounter this crisis. Now I need Your provision for it."

Jehovah Jireh will show you what that provision is, because He has preplanned it. That shouldn't be a surprise to you--especially if you are a parent. You would do the same thing for your own children, and the Lord is a far more loving parent than we could ever be.

Abraham was saying, "God already had that ram prepared for me to sacrifice. I spoke my faith, and there was my provision!"

When you speak your faith, God creates what you are speaking. After the ram was provided, Abraham said something even greater about God's provision. He said, *In the mount of the LORD it shall be seen.* (Genesis 22:14)

Some translations say, "He shall be seen." Still other translations say, "the Provision shall be seen."

What was Abraham talking about?

He was saying, "On this mountain range of Moriah, the Lord Jesus Christ shall be provided as a sacrifice for the sins of the world!'' Abraham saw the Provision which would be made for you and me.

The Bible says that Jesus Christ is the Lamb *"slain from the foundation of the world.''* (Revelation 13:8) In God's mind, He had the sacrifice of Jesus Christ already settled. He saw ahead that we would sin, and that He would need a Lamb for our redemption. God preplanned Jesus to come to earth and be His perfect sacrifice Lamb.

Abraham looked all the way forward to Jesus' physical life on this earth, and he saw God's Own Son. He saw the Lamb Who would die for the sins of the world--**Jehovah Jireh's Provision!** Jesus Himself said,

Your father Abraham rejoiced to see my day: and he saw it, and was glad. (John 8:56)

When John the Baptist saw Jesus, he said, *"Behold the Lamb of God, which taketh away the sin of the world.''* (John 1:29) He was pointing to the perfect Lamb Who would be sacrificed on Mount Calvary--in the mountain range of Moriah!

18 Forasmuch as ye know that ye were not redeemed with corruptible things, as silver and gold, from your vain conversation received by tradition from your fathers;

19 But with the precious blood of Christ, as the lamb without blemish and without spot:

20 Who verily was foreordained before the foundation of the world, but was manifest in these last times for you. (1st Peter 1:18-20)

The burnt sacrifice of consecration began with Abraham, but those lambs could only be a **covering** for sin.

91

They could never take away the sin, and the sin nature. Jesus, the Lamb of God, came to die and rise from the dead **to remove our sins**, not just cover them. He gave us brand new natures that do not want to sin.

Why?

Because God saw that is what we needed, and He gave us Jesus, His perfect Provision. That's the perfect Lamb.

The first Passover in Exodus twelve says, *"they shall take to them every man a lamb."* (Exodus 12:3) Then verse four says, *"And if the household be too little for the lamb,..."* (Exodus 12:4) Then verse five says, *"Your lamb shall be without blemish,..."* (Exodus 12:5)

The world may say, "We need a Savior;" and that's a start. The world can say, "Jesus is the Savior;" and that is true--but it's still not enough. He has to be **your** Savior, **your** Lamb, and **your Provision!**

11 And I beheld, and I heard the voice of many angels round about the throne and the beasts and the elders; and the number of them was ten thousands times ten thousand, and thousands of thousands;

12 Saying with a loud voice, Worthy is the Lamb that was slain to receive power, and riches, and wisdom, and strength, and honour, and glory, and blessing. (Revelation 5:11, 12)

Jesus is **the** Worthy Lamb--but more important, **your Worthy Lamb, and mine.** I once said to Jesus, "You are my Lamb, but the Bible also says that You are my Lion. Those two are opposites."

He told me, "You need both a Lamb, and a Lion. As a Lamb, I died to free you from the bondage of sin. As a Lion, all power is given to me that is in heaven and in earth. As King of kings, I'll give you power to walk in this life in the fullness of what the Lamb purchased for you."

Jesus is **your Lamb.** And He is **your Lion.** He is **your perfect Provision** for all you shall ever need. Praise the Lord that **Jehovah Jireh saw ahead, and made provision: He gave you Himself.**

Jehovah Jireh - Are you relying completely on Jehovah Jireh for your every provision? Do not lean unto your own understanding. Rather, realize that without Him you can do nothing. **He is your Provider--ask Him what His provision is to fill your need!**

16 For God so loved the world, that He gave his only begotten Son, that whosoever believeth in him should not perish, but have everlasting life.

17 For God sent not his Son in to the world to condemn the world; but that the world through him might be saved. (John 3:16-17)

He that spared not his own Son, but delivered him up for us all, how shall he not with him also freely give us all things? (Romans 8:32)

9 In this was manifested the love of God toward us, because that God sent his only begotten Son into the world, that we might live through him.

10 Herein is love, not that we loved God, but that he loved us, and sent his Son to be the propitiation for our sins. (1st John 4:9-10)

But my God shall supply all your need according to his riches in glory by Christ Jesus. (Philippians 4:19)

Chapter 6

JEHOVAH M'KADDESH

Have you ever had a strong desire to have your personality lined up perfectly with the Lord's personality? Jesus wants you to have a total image of Himself living through you.

He gives you that image in the name **Jehovah M'Kaddesh.** The name Jehovah M'Kaddesh is first found in Leviticus 20:7-8, and it means **"Jehovah Who Sanctifies."** This shows the Lord as One Who desires to set you apart by making your personality one with His.

7 Sanctify yourselves therefore, and be ye holy: for I am the LORD your God.

8 And ye shall keep my statutes, and do them: I am the LORD (JEHOVAH M'KADDESH) which sanctify you. (Leviticus 20:7-8)

Many Christians seem to drift here, and wander there, not really knowing God's plan for them. They know about

God. They know about the possibility of having a deeper relationship with Him. They know about the baptism of the Holy Spirit. Some are even baptized with the Holy Spirit. But there seems to be no growth, and no real hunger to grow.

Why does this happen? How can Christians go aimlessly through life, never getting involved in God's Word, never witnessing, and never being active in the Body of Christ?

It is because there is something lacking; and the key is in this name: **Jehovah M'Kaddesh.**

Leviticus tells about the people who have **already** been redeemed. It focuses upon the sanctification which ought to follow one's redemption. This book sets forth the **way** in which the Revealing One would have His people walk.

I therefore, the prisoner of the Lord, beseech you that ye walk worthy of the vocation wherewith ye are called. (Ephesians 4:1)

The term **sanctify** is a word which means "consecrate," "dedicate," or "holy." Basically, It shows Jehovah setting His people apart to walk in holiness, because He is their God. Consequently, the Lord's people were to set themselves apart to walk in total dedication to Him.

This is **Jehovah M'Kaddesh.** He is the Holy One Who demands holiness from His children.

Consider this. Even today the Jewish people are still a people who are **set apart.** When you think of the Hebrew race, what do you automatically think of? Their God! In the days of the Old Covenant, they were far more set apart then they are today, however. Jewish holidays, cer-

96

emonies, rites, social and political system--**everything** related back to their God. They were a people set apart.

There is another interesting point about Leviticus 20:7, which says to **"sanctify yourselves."** God did not do all of the sanctifying. Within the personality of Jehovah M'Kaddesh lies the truth that men must choose holiness.

Although it has been commanded by the Lord that we are to set ourselves apart, He will never force us to do so. One man who put off making that choice was named King Nebuchadnezzar of Babylon.

Throughout his life, Nebuchadnezzar received many indications from the Lord, Who wanted to be Master of his life--in total control. One of the first indications came when three Hebrew captive children would not eat the food eaten by Nebuchadnezzar's students.

They received permission to eat a diet of **pulse**, which is a vegetable and lentil mixture. The condition for their being allowed to eat this food was, "At the end of ten days, if we don't look better and healthier than the other boys after eating this food, we will switch back and eat your food."

The eunuch in charge had agreed, and at the end of the allotted time period, the boys looked better than anyone else. The eunuch was so impressed with their appearance that he let them continue eating the pulse.

At the same time, the consecration which these Hebrew children made had wonderful effects upon their relationship with the Lord. He said, "Because you have been faithful and obedient to Me, I will make you ten times wiser than the other wise men."

This was the first witness of their God's attempts to win over Nebuchadnezzar. When they appeared before him and tested their wisdom against all other wise men, the Hebrew children's wisdom far surpassed all others. That was the first sign to Nebuchadnezzar.

Directly after the Hebrew children obtained this wisdom, something else happened.

1 And in the second year of the reign of Nebuchadnezzar, Nebuchadnezzar dreamed dreams, wherewith his spirit was troubled, and his sleep brake from him.

2 Then the king commanded to call the magicians, and the astrologers, and the sorcerers, and the Chaldeans, for to shew the king his dreams. So they came and stood before the king. (Daniel 2:1-2)

Nebuchadnezzar had dreamed about a very strange image. After he was startled awake from it, he could not remember what the dream was. All he knew was that he must know what it meant.

He said, "I must know what I dreamed," and called for all of the country's "wise men." The men were not actually wise--they were all involved with the occult. When they went before the king, he commanded them, "Tell me what I have dreamed."

"Impossible!" they said. "It cannot be done!"

Nebuchadnezzar was furious with this display of ignorance in his so-called wise men. He warned them, "If you do not tell me what I dreamed, I shall have you all killed!"

Daniel soon heard that their lives were on the line, so he prayed to God, saying, "Reveal to us what King Nebuchadnezzar has dreamed, and show us the interpretation."

God revealed both the dream and its meaning to Daniel. The next morning he went before the king and told him what God had revealed. This was God's second dealing with King Nebuchadnezzar.

Nebuchadnezzar was so turned on to hear the dream and its interpretation that he said,

Of a truth it is, that your God is a God of gods, and a Lord of kings, and a revealer of secrets, seeing thou couldest reveal this secret. (Daniel 2:47)

Upon hearing the Word of God from Daniel, Nebuchadnezzar had a knowledge of the Triune Godhead, and he still was not saved. With a revelation like that, one would think that he would become excited about serving God--but he didn't. His spirit had not yet awakened to the things of the Lord.

Many times, we may try to bring our intellects and bodies in line with God, while our spirit is not in line.

It doesn't work that way! In fact, God works in a very opposite order than our human reasoning. First of all, He wants our spirit to be sanctified, set apart unto Him. Then He wants to renew our intellect to His Word, and renew our emotions to His Word. Renewed spirits bring renewed souls which are full of God's Word. Then, God's Word brings faith, and our bodies line up with His Word.

Some people wouldn't ever dream of committing adultery, or smoking or drinking. They've lined their bodies up with God. But they'll think nothing of fighting with other Christians and harboring an ugly attitude toward their pastor. They are rebellious, and have big personality problems for one reason: while their body and soul are "lined up," their spirit is not!

All three must be sanctified: spirit first, then soul and body.

Nebuchadnezzar needed to have his soul renewed. For although He had said, **"your God"** to Daniel, he hadn't called the Lord **"my God."**

Over a period of time, Nebuchadnezzar built a huge stone idol of himself. It was huge--ninety feet tall and nine feet around. It stood on the plain of Dura, where nothing else could obstruct the view. Then Nebuchadnezzar said;

4 ...To you it is commanded, O people, nations, and languages,

5 That at what time ye hear the sound of the cornet, flute, harp, sackbut, psaltery, dulcimer, and all kinds of musick, ye fall down and worship the golden image that Nebuchadnezzar the king hath set up:

6 And whoso falleth not down and worshippeth shall the same hour be cast into the midst of a burning fiery furnace. (Daniel 3:4-6)

Meanwhile, because Daniel had accurately interpreted Nebuchadnezzar's dream, he and the other wise Hebrew children had been placed in positions of leadership. They would soon be required by the king's law to bow to his idol on the plain of Dura, but they could not.

They knew that there was only one God, the living God, Jehovah, Elohim.

They refused to bow, and when Nebuchadnezzar heard this, he was very angry. Here were the leaders setting a terrible example by usurping his orders!

God had dealt with Nebuchadnezzar, but he had now forgotten all about that. He was only concerned with punishing the rebels who would not bow to his idol. He was so angry that he made the fire even hotter than normal temperature. The men who threw them in were consumed by the escaping flames. Before Nebuchadnezzar had thrown them in, the three Hebrews told him, "Our God is able to deliver us; but no matter what, we won't bow."

Although the three were bound with rope and thrown into this furnace, when Nebuchadnezzar looked in, this is what he saw:

Lo, I see four men loose, walking in the midst of the fire, and they have no hurt; and the form of the fourth is like the Son of God. (Daniel 3:25)

That convinced Nebuchadnezzar that these three Hebrew children knew something he hadn't known. He issued a decree which said, "Anyone who says anything against their God will have their house made into a dung hill. He is the only God who can deliver people like this!"

But the king was still speaking with his intellect. He would still not be set apart, for he had not allowed God to sanctify his spirit.

Then one night, Nebuchadnezzar dreamed another dream, but this time he remembered it. It bothered him just as the previous dream had. He called Daniel in and said:

10 Thus were the visions of mine head in my bed; I saw, and behold a tree in the midst of the earth, and the height thereof was great.

11 The tree grew, and was strong, and the height thereof reached unto heaven, and the sight thereof to the end of all the earth:

12 The leaves thereof were fair, and the fruit thereof much, and in it was meat for all: the beasts of the field had shadow under it, and the fowls of the heaven dwelt in the boughs thereof, and all flesh was fed of it.

13 I saw in the visions of my head upon my bed, and, behold a watcher and an holy one came down from heaven;

14 He cried aloud, and said thus, Hew down the tree, and cut off his branches, shake off his leaves, and scatter his fruit: let the beasts get away from under it, and the fowls from his branches:

15 Nevertheless leave the stump of his roots in the earth, even with a band of iron and brass, in the tender grass of the field; and let it be wet with the dew of heaven, and let his portion be with the beasts in the grass of the earth:

16 Let his heart be changed from man's and let a beast's heart be given unto him: and let seven times pass over him. (Daniel 4:10-16)

Daniel interpreted Nebuchadnezzar's dream. "This has been established, and it will happen unless you change your ways. You have lifted yourself up on pride and believed that you are the supreme one, when it is God Who has given this kingdom to you. The tree represents your kingdom. And if you do not repent, it shall be cut down to the stump. Worst of all, if you do not humble yourself, you are going to lose your mind for seven years, and you will think you are an animal, and live like one."

But Nebuchadnezzar did not listen to Daniel. In his mind, he knew Daniel's God was the true God--but he would not receive it in his spirit. Nebuchadnezzar did not want to set himself apart unto God.

A year later, the king stepped out onto his balcony to survey his vast empire. He said, "Look at this great empire which I have built." And at that moment, King Nebuchadnezzar went stark, raving mad. The people of his palace had to have him kept in the palace gardens, because he imagined himself to be an animal.

For seven years, Nebuchadnezzar's hair grew long, and his nails grew long, and he crawled about and barked as if he were an animal.

Seven years passed by, and at the end of that time, Nebuchadnezzar's heart became transformed.

And at the end of the days I Nebuchadnezzar lifted up mine eyes unto heaven, and mine understanding returned unto me, and I blessed the most High, and I praised and honoured him that liveth for ever, whose dominion is an everlasting dominion, and his kingdom is from generation to generation: (Daniel 4:34)

When the king, who had lived as a beast for seven years, acknowledged that God was the Supreme One, his sanity returned. Nebuchadnezzar sanctified himself unto God. And when his spirit came in line with the Lord, what happened? His mind, intellect, reasoning, and physical body changed from being like an animal's. He became a man of God!

For this is the will of God, even your sanctification. (1st Thessalonians 4:3a)

This verse talks about keeping your entire spirit, soul, and body blameless unto the second coming of our Lord Jesus Christ. God doesn't want you to have little hidden closets and missed motivations. He wants you to be totally set apart unto Him. **This is what JEHOVAH M'KADDESH is all about.**

How can you sanctify yourself?

Through relying totally on Him in EVERYTHING!

In the book of Leviticus, moral and spiritual purity can only be preserved through sanctification--a setting apart. Why does the name Jehovah M'Kaddesh appear over seven hundred times throughout the Bible? Because God wants a people who are set apart unto Him.

1 And the Lord spake unto Moses, saying,

2 Sanctify unto me all the first born. (Exodus 13:1-2)

Jehovah had already said, "Israel is My son, even My first born." He had set apart the children of Israel and made them His own. When redemption from sin came, it **set them apart.**

When Jesus Christ redeemed you from sin, and the law of sin and death, what should happen? You should be set apart, sanctified from the rest of creation. Jesus, the firstborn of many brethren, wants you to be set apart, **in Him!**

God also set apart a special day, in which people were not to work--they were only to honor him: the Sabbath. A firstborn, a nation, a Sabbath, were all sanctified unto the Lord. Israel's great feasts and fasts, with all of their spiritual and dispensational significance, were celebrated and set apart for the Lord.

A special year was ushered in after seven sabbath years, which would proclaim redemption and liberty for all, the year of Jubilee. Every seven years, an entire **year** was sanctified unto JEHOVAH M'KADDESH!

When you belong to God, you have been set apart. But you are not just set apart to serve Him with your flesh. You're not just set apart to serve Him with your mind. That alone won't cut it. You must be set apart to serve Him in Spirit and in truth!

God called Jonah to be a prophet, and he did prophesy successfully to a certain king. Then God told Jonah to prophesy to Nineveh and tell them to repent. But Jonah had a problem: mixed motivations! He wanted to obey God's call only when it suited him. Although he loved God with all of his mind, his spirit was not set apart. He did not want to call his nation's enemies to repentance. He wanted God to destroy them, instead.

Instead of going east as the Lord had instructed him, Jonah headed west, and was swallowed by a great fish. It wasn't until Jonah had some time to think things over, inside of the fish, that he totally consecrated himself, spirit and all, unto the Lord.

A humbled man, Jonah went to Nineveh and preached one message: "REPENT!" The people of Nineveh said, "We want to repent." And they were spared. But instead of being happy about the peoples' repentance, Jonah went right back to being the person he was before. He sat under a vine and cried because God didn't destroy the people. Why? Because his spirit had not been **sanctified!** He did not call upon Jehovah M'Kaddesh, the One Who sanctifies.

What is wrong with Christians who aren't totally set apart unto God? They don't know **Jehovah M'Kaddesh**.

Some individuals in the Bible were actually set apart from their very birth to belong to the Lord. Jeremiah was sanctified to serve Jehovah as a prophet to the nations-- and his being set apart happened while he was still in his mother's womb. John the Baptist was set apart while he was still in Elizabeth's womb.

Why should Christians be set apart? Because Jehovah is set apart! He has said, "There is none beside Me; there is none as holy as Jehovah." Because He is set apart, His people must be set apart. If you belong to God, you shouldn't be like everyone else--you should be sanctified, different! The key verse in Leviticus, which teaches you how to approach a holy God and walk in a manner which He approves, says, ...*for I the LORD our God am holy.* (Leviticus 19:2)

God's holiness changed Isaiah's life. He saw seraphim surrounding God's throne, saying, "Holy, holy is Jehovah of hosts."

God asked, "Who will go for us?"

And Isaiah made the decision; "Send me!"

The holiness of God totally awed, inspired and changed Isaiah. It caused him to set apart his spirit, his soul, and his body unto the Lord. He wanted his life to be complete and whole before Jehovah M'Kaddesh.

Even God's Spirit is called the Holy Spirit. David prayed to the Lord in Psalm 51:11, "...take not thy holy spirit from me." God's Spirit is holy. How can you not allow yourself to be set apart, when the Spirit of He Who is set apart lives inside you? A Holy Spirit shouldn't live inside an unholy vessel. God's holiness very clearly contrasts the heathen deities--their impurity and corruption of nature and worship.

Israel was commanded again and again, "You shall have no other gods before Me."

Why?

Because **Jehovah is set apart.** Those idols were not really gods, and the Bible says that idols are a thing of nought. How can you line up with nothing?

God's holiness was seen by Moses and the children of Israel at the Red Sea when they sang a song: *Who is like unto thee, O LORD.* (Exodus 15:11) The very same song is in Revelation 15:3.

3b Great and marvellous are thy works, Lord God Almighty; just and true are thy ways, thou King of saints.

4a Who shall not fear thee, O Lord, and glorify thy name? for thou only art holy: (Revelation 15:3b-4a)

Glory dwells within holiness. The cry of the seraphim who veil their eyes in the presence of God's holiness is "Holy, holy, holy, is the Lord of hosts." The word "holiness" confuses many people, but I like to think of it this way. When you set yourself apart unto God, you will be **whole**--you will be holy.

When I was a young girl, I had a cousin who was very beautiful, but her parents dressed her in very dull and plain clothes. They pulled her hair back into a severe style.

I discovered they did that because they wanted her to be holy. To some people, holiness is captured in the outward appearance. But it is much more that that. God calls us to be modest, but He doesn't call us to look funny, strange or unattractive. He just wants us to be **complete**, starting with our spirits.

When your spirit is in right relationship with God, your soul and body will line up. Really, your soul and body are just things that your spirit **wears. Holiness, a setting apart,** begins with the wholeness of God inside of you. Some people are incomplete because they've never known and received **Jehovah M'Kaddesh,** who **is** wholeness itself.

9 For in him dwelleth all the fulness of the God-head bodily.

10 And ye are complete in him, which is the head of all principality and power: (Colossians 2:9-10)

Since God has given you a free will in your sanctification, He will never force His will upon you. You must be willing for your spirit to line up with His Spirit.

Sometimes I find that I am unwilling. You may encounter the same problem.

What can be done?

I have found that the best way to counter those feelings is to go before Him and **pray** to make me willing!

From Jesus' very conception, He was holy. Mary carried His holy seed within her body before His birth. When Jesus was born, He was clean. His spirit, soul and body were one-hundred percent in line with His Father, God. Jesus actually became our sanctification when He offered Himself once and for all. Are you willing to wear His sanctification? It is the very sanctification of Jehovah M'Kaddesh!

15 But as he which hath called you is holy, so be ye holy in all manner of conversation;

16 Because it is written, Be ye holy; for I am holy. (1st Peter 1:15-16)

What is holiness? What effect does sanctification have?

But ye are a chosen generation, a royal priesthood, an holy nation, a peculiar people, that ye should shew forth the praises of him who hath called you out of darkness into his marvellous light: (1st Peter 2:9)

When you sanctify yourself by walking in Jesus' Own sanctification, you will shine brilliantly to the world. You can't help but be a light of the Gospel. Showing holiness isn't long dresses, dark stockings, and hair in a knot. Some people who wear long dresses have tongues as sharp as razors. Some have nasty spirits, because they are only separated on the outside, not holy on the inside.

On the inside of your spirit dwells a new man who looks like Jesus. When you let him take over, he'll line up the rest of you. The Bible says in First Corinthians:

> *And such were some of you: but ye are washed,*
> *but ye are sanctified, but ye are justified in the*
> *name of the Lord Jesus, and by the Spirit of our*
> *God.* (1st Corinthians 6:11)

Ephesians 4:24 tells you to *put on the new man,*
which after God is created in righteousness and true
holiness. Don't try to work up your own holiness--you
don't have it! Set yourself apart in the holiness of Jesus.
The Bible says that when we see Him, we shall be like
Him, and that even this very **hope** will purify us.

How can you see the One Who sanctifies?

In His Word! Do you want to know God's perfect will
for your personality today? He wants it to be sanctified!

God wants you to be **set apart unto Him,** just as He
has set you apart. He wants to make you like Himself,
spirit, soul and body, so that you will be blameless upon
the coming of our Lord Jesus Christ!

JEHOVAH M'KADDESH - He desires you to be like Himself--set apart in His Own righteousness and holiness. What more beautiful robes could you wear? The perfect personality is one which is consecrated to being totally like Him: the One Who sanctifies, JEHOVAH M'KADDESH.

Thus saith the LORD the King of Israel, and his redeemer the LORD of hosts; I am the first, and I am the last; and beside me there is no God. (Isaiah 44:6)

There is none holy as the LORD: for there is none beside thee. (1   Samuel 2:2)

One thing have I desired of the LORD, that will I seek after; that I may dwell in the house of the LORD all the days of my life, to behold the beauty of the LORD, and to inquire in his temple. (Psalm 27:4)

And let the beauty of the LORD our God be upon us: and establish thou the work of our hands upon us; yea, the work of our hands establish thou it. (Psalm 90:17)

Whereby are given unto us exceeding great and precious promises: that by these ye might be partakers of the divine nature, having escaped the corruption that is in the world through lust. (2nd Peter 1:4)

Chapter 7

JEHOVAH NISSI

When you look at your image in Christ Jesus, you must look only at the image which is victorious! I don't know what your weak areas are, but I know that Jesus can overcome them to make you a victor and a conqueror. God's Word says that Jesus always causes you to triumph in Him. **You must see yourself as being only IN HIM!** Without Him you can do nothing. But with Him, all things are possible!

Jehovah Nissi actually means "Jehovah, my Banner." You are going to discover just how God revealed Himself this way. This name is found for the first time in Exodus 17:15, during a time when the children of Israel were becoming acquainted with the Lord.

He is a mighty God! He had sent the plagues upon Egypt and delivered His People in a miraculous way. They had met Jehovah as a Victorious One, step by step, in every experience and situation.

Only a few weeks had passed from Jehovah's revealing Himself in a brand new way when the Israelites "forgot" all that He had been to them. They came out of a land called Marah, through a place called Elim, and into a land called "the wilderness of sin." They actually began sinning, too, by murmuring against Moses, because there wasn't any food. Then Jehovah appeared in a cloud of glory, and fed them with wilderness manna. Manna must have been wonderfully nutritious food, because that is all that God's people ate. It supplied **all** of their nutritional needs.

After the Lord gave the Israelites manna, they traveled on to a place called Rephidim. (Exodus 17) At Rephidim there was no water at all, and the people thirsted terribly. Hunger may be difficult and discouraging, but thirst brings unbearable suffering and torment. Finally, the desperate people began threatening Moses and doubting God. They forgot all of the miraculous provisions which He had given them: the parting of the Red Sea, the drowning of the Pharaoh and his host, the manna, and God's presence through the pillars of cloud and fire. They said, "Is the Lord among us or not?"

The Lord certainly was among them. He told Moses to strike a rock in the land of Horeb (which means "fresh inspiration"), and it brought forth enough water to quench the multitude's thirst.

The New Testament tells you that a Rock which provided water in the wilderness was Christ--He followed them throughout their entire journey. Sometimes the children of Israel had to dig for water. Another time they had to sing to the earth where they dug. But inevitably, water would come bubbling up from the earth.

Eventually, the Israelites came against a terrible foe, whose name was Amalek. The Amalekites were not the sweetest people in the world, even though Amalek was Esau's grandson, according to Genesis 36:12. The Amalekites were direct descendants of Isaac, but they became a terrible enemy to Israel--a real thorn in the flesh, who menaced their spiritual and national life.

The Amalekites were the first nation to oppose Israel. They were both numerous and powerful. As closely related as they were to the Israelites, I would have thought that they would offer support.

Instead, they opposed God's people at every turn, in mean and cowardly ways. For instance, the Amalekites would not attack Israel's fighting men--instead, they would wait and attack the weaker ones at the end of the line--the faint, the weary, the elderly. The Amalekites were unscrupulous and vicious, and God's face was against them.

> ...*thou shalt blot out the remembrance of Amalek from under heaven.* (Deuteronomy 25:19)
>
> *14 And the LORD said unto Moses, Write this for a memorial in a book, and rehearse it in the ears of Joshua: for I will utterly put out the rememberance of Amalek from under heaven.*
>
> *15 And Moses built an altar, and called the name of it Jehovah-nissi:*
>
> *16 For he said, Because the LORD hath sworn that the LORD will have war with Amalek from*

generation to generation. (Exodus 17:14-16)

Jehovah swore that He would war against Amalek from generation to generation.

Why?

Because Jehovah is righteous, and He hated the sin of the Amalekites. He wanted to cut their memory off from the earth.

Generations after this incident at Rephidim, which we will discuss further, King Saul was commissioned to wipe the Amalekites off the face of the earth. But King Saul's greed got the best of him, and he disobeyed God. It is interesting to note that, in the end, an Amalekite killed Saul.

Why?

Because he spared what he should not have spared. What the devil tries to put in your lives must be dealt with and destroyed. If you don't kill it, it may return and kill you.

The Amalekites were living near Rephidim, tending their own flocks and herds. They hated the Israelites in the first place, but they were also very jealous to them, so they decided to fight them. When the Amalekites came against the children of Israel, finally the children of Israel did not fall apart. They were not a well-trained army, as were the Amalekites, but they were finally learning to place their trust in the Lord.

A man named Joshua was standing by, and his name appropriately meant, "Jehovah is our help, or salvation." Moses called to Joshua saying, "I want you to be in command over the army when the Amalekites come."

God told Moses to stand at the top of a nearby hill with his hands held up. Moses climbed to the hilltop and held up the rod of God which had wrought many miracles.

11 And it came to pass when Moses held up his hand that Israel prevailed: and when he let down his hand, Amalek prevailed.

12 But Moses' hands were heavy; and they took a stone, and put it under him, and he sat thereon; and Aaron and Hur stayed up his hands, the one on the one side, and the other on the other side; and his hands were steady until the going down of the sun.

13 And Joshua discomfited Amalek and his people with the edge of the sword. (Exodus 17:11-13)

As long as Moses held his hands up in the air, Israel was conquering. But when his arms grew weary, and he lowered them, Amalek would begin to conquer. The fact that Moses' men, Aaron and Hur, brought him support and stayed his hands in the air shows something beautiful.

They didn't say, "That Moses! Just when we start winning, he gets tired. Why doesn't he get tough?"

No! They **supported** him.. When you see brothers and sisters in the Lord growing weary or faint, it's your job to restore them! Be a support to them. If you sow it in someone else's life, you'll reap it in your own.

In Moses' hand was the miracle-working rod of God which had brought terrible plagues upon the land of Egypt. That same rod had closed the waters behind the Israelites and drowned the pursuing Pharaoh and host.

This rod of God was more that a mere rod. It was the rod of God's mighty hand: the rod of Elohim!

Moses was holding up **the banner of God which brought them victory!** Moses was carrying **a symbol of God's presence.** As long as God's presence was established as the high standard, the Israelites prevailed in battle.

When you hear the word **banner**, although you probably picture a flag, that is not necessarily what a banner was in Moses' day. It was a bare pole with a bright and shining ornament which would glitter in the sun when held high in the air.

The word for banner actually means **"to glisten, a pole or ensign, a standard, or a miracle."** The banner or **standard** represented God's cause. It was **a symbol of His deliverance and mighty salvation** which caused His people to be victors over their enemies.

When the Israelites used the words "Lift up," or rise up," they were using the literal word "banner." **Jehovah Nissi is the Lord--Israel's banner and YOUR banner; Israel's victory and YOUR victory!**

Who is **Jehovah Nissi?**

He is the Lord, our Victory!

While Joshua was out fighting to bring forth Jehovah's salvation, the rod of Elohim was held aloft in Moses' hand. With the Lord's banner held high, there was victory.

As long as you say, "God is the Victorious One in my life," you will be on top of your circumstances. But when you drop your hands and say, "I'm defeated, the devil has me down," you can count on defeat. Focus your eyes on the Lord, Jehovah Nissi, and keep your hands up in the air, holding His victorious standard high!

Israel's war against the Amalekites is an example of our own spiritual warfare. The Bible says we have a battle going on--even against our **own** flesh, not to mention against Satan.

The flesh lusts against the spirit, and the spirit against the flesh. But although your members may "war" against each others' desires, and battles are going on, God wants you to be victorious!

That's why He gave you His Spirit to live within you. God is not a loser, and you should not be either.

God told Moses to stand on top of the hill when Joshua and the army fought the battle against Amalek. When I read that, it reminded me of Ephesians 6:11-17.

11 Put on the whole armour of God, that ye may be able to stand against the wiles of the devil.

12 For we wrestle not against flesh and blood, but against principalities, against powers, against the rulers of the darkness of this world, against spiritual wickedness in high places.

*13 Wherefore take unto you the whole armour of God, that ye may be able to **withstand** in the evil day, and having done all, to **stand.***

*14 **Stand** therefore, having your loins girt about with truth, and having on the breastplate of righteousness;*

15 And your feet shod with the preparation of the gospel of peace;

119

16 Above all, taking the shield of faith, wherewith ye shall be able to quench all the fiery darts of the wicked.

17 And take the helmet of salvation, and the sword of the Spirit, which is the word of God. (Ephesians 6:11-17)

God did not tell you to fight in your own armor. He gave you His armor. And if you'll wear it and stand in it, He will put you over! He's the Lord, your Banner.

2 Lift ye up a banner upon the high mountain . . .

3 I have commanded my sanctified ones . . . even them that rejoice in my highness.

4 The noise of a multitude in the mountains, like as of a great people; a tumultuous noise of the kingdoms of nations gathered together: the Lord of hosts mustereth the host of the battle.

11 And I will punish the world for their evil, and the wicked for their iniquity . . . (Isaiah 13:2-4, 11)

Righteous Jehovah hates sin. If you will hold high His standard of victory, sin will not overtake you. Other people may come against you with evil, but you are supposed to conquer with good!

Why? Because **you are standing tall in the armor of Jehovah Nissi, your Victor, your Champion.** Jesus did not promise you, "Well, now that I've taken the victory, it's going to be a piece of cake for you." You have to **stand**--but if you will, He did promise that not even the very gates of hell itself could prevail against you! He has made you a victor in Himself .

Ephesians six says that you are not supposed to wrestle against flesh and blood. Always remember, God does not give you His armor to fight against people.

If you are fighting against people, you're going to lose. You wrestle against principalities, powers, rulers of darkness in this world, and spiritual wickedness in high places. Do you want to be a victor against them? **Then stand against them in the armor of Jehovah Nissi!** To wear His armor, you cannot lean to your own understanding; you have to lean on His Word!

There is no question that Christians encounter spiritual battles, but you are not supposed to lie down and say, "All right, you win."

God says, "you're not a loser! **I am Jehovah Nissi:** your Banner, your Miracle, your Victory, Who **makes** you a winner." That's why you are fighting a good fight of faith. It's good, because you win, in the Lord!

Thou therefore endure hardness, as a good soldier of Jesus Christ. (2nd Timothy 2:3)

The word 'enduring means "to hold onto God's Word," and "to stand fast in faith." Why doesn't Ephesians six give you any armor to wear on your back? Because you have **Jehovah Nissi** to go **before** you into the battle! Because He wants to be your victory!

You are not fighting battles in your own strength; you're in His strength. When you allow that strength which is in you to flow by relying on Him as your Banner, then you will overcome.

121

Two men who discovered this were men by the names of Joshua and Caleb. When the Israelites were to take the Promised Land, Moses sent Joshua and Caleb to spy out the land. Actually, he sent along ten other men with them. I think Joshua and Caleb were the only two who mattered. When all of the men returned, the report of those two men was wonderful. "We **can** take the Promised Land! **We can do it!**"

The other ten men said, "There is no way that we'll take the land! There are giants in there, and the walls reach to the sky. Those giants would eat us like meat!"

Why were the ten men so defeated in their attitude? Because **they were not looking to Jehovah Nissi** to enter the land before them. They were not considering the fact that God had already promised them that land.

Joshua and Caleb said, "Those giants are like grasshoppers! They are nothing to us!"

How could they be so bold?

They were both considering the circumstances in light of God's Word. They were on top, looking down. Those other ten spies had the wrong self-image. They saw themselves as defeated ones, not victorious ones. They did not see their miracle-working God, or His promises. All they could see was giants.

Joshua and Caleb saw their own true images in God. They said, "We are already **victorious because of Jehovah Nissi, our powerful, Almighty God!**"

Which way do you look at it? Do you consider defeat? Or do you look to the Victorious One?

After the ten spies gave a negative report, the people began to murmur and complain, saying, "We cannot take the Promised Land. If we try, our little children will die there."

What happened? God refused to let them enter the land, because they were not looking to Him as their **Jehovah Nissi.** All of those people died without entering the land of Promise, and their children entered the land after they had all died off. The ten spies said, "We cannot go in," and they didn't. The people said, "We can't go in," and they didn't go in either. Joshua and Caleb had said, "We can go in. We can take the land." And they were the only ones of that generation who did enter! They knew Jehovah Nissi, their Banner, their Victorious One.

After the people had groaned and moaned, and Moses had reproved them, they said, We changed our minds. We'll go in and defeat them!"

Moses said, "It's too late now. Don't go up, because Jehovah is not among you." But the people went into the land anyway.

What happened? They were defeated, and chased by the Amalekites. You cannot win in your own strength. You can only win in God's strength.

After Moses' death, the Israelites had a battle inside the Promised Land when they took the City of Jericho in a tremendous victory. But then they went to take a city called Ai, and they lost the battle.

Why did they lose? Because they did not ask God how to take the city.

They didn't wait on Him to see His divine military plan. Instead, they raced in and were defeated. When this happened, Joshua fell on his face before God.

"God!" he cried, "Why did we lose?"

God said, "There is sin in the camp. You'd better get rid of it, or I won't go anywhere with you." (That was Jehovah, angry with sin.) Joshua got to the root of the problem immediately! He said, "Get right with the Lord!" and he straightened out the situation. Then they went to Ai again, and God made them victorious in battle! God went before them as Jehovah Nissi.

You will not win in your own strength. You can only win through God's strength and with His plan. In fact, if you receive His victory and walk in it, the Bible says that you've **already won**, in Him, because Jesus has defeated the enemy!

> *3 Hear, O Israel, ye approach this day unto battle against your enemies: let not your hearts faint, fear not, and do not tremble, neither be ye terrified because of them;*
>
> *4 For the LORD your God is he that goeth with you, to fight for you against your enemies, to save you.* (Deuteronomy 20:3-4)
>
> *The LORD is on my side; I will not fear: what can man do unto me?* (Psalm 118:6)

What are these scriptures saying? They are saying, "I've already won, because I have **Jehovah Nissi** on my side! He is my Victorious One!" The rod in Moses' hand was much more than a symbol. Moses named one of his altars after the rod. He called it, **"Jehovah Nissi."** He was saying, "He is my Victorious One, my Banner." Generations later, the prophet Isaiah spoke about this rod.

> *1 And there shall come forth a rod out of the stem of Jesse, and a Branch shall grow out of*

his roots:

10 And in that day there shall be a root of Jesse, which shall stand for an ensign (banner) of the people. (Isaiah 11:1,10)

That Rod, that Stem, came from the lineage of King David of Israel's father, Jesse.

Who is the Rod?

He is Jesus Christ, born of the seed of David, according to the flesh.

The Lord told Moses to lift up a serpent in the wilderness, after the people had been bitten by poisonous snakes. He told Moses that all of the people who would look on the serpent which was being held up would be healed from their affliction.

The word used for **pole,** on which the serpent was lifted up, is **"banner."** The Lord Jesus said, *"As Moses lifted up the serpent in the wilderness, even so must the Son of man be lifted up."* (John 3:14) Jesus was lifted up on the banner--the cross. That very cross is not a sign of defeat--it is a sign of victory! The cross of Christ is our banner, our strength which He has already won.

Jesus said, *"...In the world ye shall have tribulation: but be of good cheer; I have overcome the world."* And in Hebrews 13:5 He says, *"...I will never leave thee...."* And *"...lo, I am with you alway, even unto the end of the world."* (Matthew 28:20)

When you place your faith in the Rod, you can be assured of victory, because First John 5:4 says, *"For whatsoever is born of God overcometh the world: and this is the victory that overcometh the world, even our faith."*

Jesus is at the Father's right hand in heavenly places, far above all principality, power, might, and dominion, and every names that is named. (Ephesians 1:20-21)

And hath raised us up together, and made us sit together in heavenly places in Christ Jesus. (Ephesians 2:6)

31 ...If God be for us, who can be against us?

37 ...we are more than conquerors through him that loved us. (Romans 8:31,37)

Jesus is your Banner--Jehovah, Jesus! You go from strength to strength, from faith to faith, from glory to glory in Him. First Corinthians 15:57 does not say that you can win only part of the time. It doesn't tell you that you'll only be a part-time conqueror.

Many people plan to fail. When I studied the Parable of the Sower and saw the hundred-fold, sixty-fold, and thirty-fold returns, I tried to be sweet and humble. I said, "Oh, Lord, I'd be satisfied with just a thirty- fold return."

He said, "Well then you want seventy-fold failure. Why don't you take one hundred-fold, the whole victory? That's what My Word promises."

But thanks be to God, which giveth us the victory through our Lord Jesus Christ. (1st Corinthians 15:57)

Now thanks be unto God, which always causeth us to triumph in Christ.... (2nd Corinthians 2:14)

He did not say that you can triumph only in a few situations. He said that in Him, you're always a victorious one! You are supposed to conquer, because Jesus is a Conqueror! You may think, "I'm not very righteous," and think that you aren't the best Christian, because you've sinned. But you can repent from sin and stand fully dressed in the beautiful armor of the Victorious One!

Jesus took all of your sins upon Himself, and He gave you His righteousness. I like this comparison. When a lamb dies, the shepherd removes the lamb's skin and places it upon an orphan lamb. Then the mother lamb, who has lost her baby, smells her baby's skin on the orphaned lamb. Because of the skin which is draped over him, she'll adopt and raise that baby as her own.

It's the same way with Jesus' righteousness. When He died, He clothed you with a robe of His Own right-standing with God Almighty. It's a garment that smells like Jesus! When the Father looks at you, what does He see? He sees you, clothed in Jesus!

You have been given everything you need for victory, in Jesus Christ. He is your Banner of Victory. You can now rest in His Word and know that Jehovah Nissi desires to go before you and make you a winner.

You can be victorious even when you pass through the valley of the shadow of death, because it leads into the presence of the Father! You can sit down at His banqueting table, because every trial you encounter leads to a banquet of triumph. And then, the Father will anoint you with oil, right in the very presence of your enemies.

Your enemies cannot hurt you, because you serve **Jehovah Nissi!** He is your protection. I'm glad that we do not have to suffer defeats. Don't ever see yourself as defeated. See the devil as defeated.

The next time you see your face in the mirror, say, "I'm in Jesus Christ! I'm in Jehovah, and He is in me. So therefore, I'm a victorious one!"

Chapter 8

JEHOVAH ROPHE

It is very important that you see the revelation of Jehovah's names in their context. Exodus fifteen gives the context of how the name **Jehovah Rophe** was revealed.

When God spoke to Moses and said, *"I Am that I am,"* (Exodus 3:14) He was saying, "Whatever you may need is exactly what I am." Throughout Moses's life, as God met his needs in various ways, God would add names to His Name Jehovah.

The name **Jehovah Rophe** actually means **"Jehovah heals,"** and it arises from one of the earliest situations in the wilderness. **Jehovah Rophe** was another way of God revealing His ways: His ways of healing.

God will give you continuous revelations of Himself throughout your life. None of us have arrived. He is always fresh and new. The more I am in His Word, and the more I wait upon Him, the greater I understand Who He is in me, through me, to me, and for me! Don't ever get stale in the Word. Stay with it. Each revelation which you receive will always be more marvelous, more personal, sweeter, and more precious than the last one.

So Moses brought Israel from the Red sea, and they went out into the wilderness of Shur; and they went three days in the wilderness, and found no water. (Exodus 15:22)

At this time of their lives, the Israelites traveled by following a pillar of cloud by day, and of fire by night. They did not move unless the cloud moved, because the Lord was the Director of all their activity, and His presence was in the cloud. When the cloud would begin to lift and move, they would follow it.

When the cloud settled down, they would stop and make their resting place. The children of Israel did not wander aimlessly through the wilderness, choosing any direction that they wanted--the Lord led them.

In this passage of scripture from Exodus 15:22, you see that the cloud had led these people for three days, and during this time, there had been no water to be found. That sounds awful!

You may think, when you enter tough circumstances, that you're out of God's will. But you may be totally in His will without realizing it. The devil could be trying to slap you around a little bit to keep you from accomplishing the will of God.

If you measure whether you are in God's will by your circumstances, you'll miss it. In the book of Acts, Paul was in a shipwreck. Was he out of God's will?

Certainly not! He was supposed to go to Rome, and the devil was fighting that.

Don't let circumstances push you around. You push circumstances around.

The Israelites hadn't traveled for three days on their own, yet the Lord was leading them to places where there was no water available.

Why?

Because He wanted them to know that He would provide for them in every way.

No matter what you are going into, God will provide for you and bring you out smelling like a rose--if you'll let Him.

Did the Israelites know about Jehovah Jireh? They must have known Him, because Jehovah Jireh had been revealed in Abraham's time. These stories had been repeated again and again to the Israelites. Moses knew Jehovah Jireh. But the Israelites panicked because of their sense knowledge. Imagine hearing your children and animals crying for water. Of course, it was a very difficult time.

When the children of Israel arrived at **Marah,** which means "bitter," they found a huge pool of water, but it tasted terribly bitter. Then the people began murmuring against Moses because they could not drink the water. It certainly wasn't his fault! Moses could have said, "Shut up!" and told the Lord, "I'm tired of this crowd of murmurers!" But he didn't.

25 ...He cried unto the LORD; and the LORD shewed him a tree, which when he had cast into

131

*the waters, the waters were made sweet: there
he made for them a statute and an ordinance,
and there he proved them,*

*26 And said, If thou wilt diligently harken to
the voice of the LORD thy God, and wilt do that
which is right in his sight, and wilt give ear to
his commandments, and keep all his statutes,
I will put none of these diseases upon thee,
which I have brought upon the Egyptians: for
I am the LORD that healeth thee.* (Exodus
15:25-26)

Moses threw a tree into the water. This is significant.
Action must accompany faith. You can talk faith, but you
must **walk** it, also. When Moses threw the tree in, the
water was sweetened, and Jehovah revealed Himself to
His people in a new way. He said, **"I am Jehovah
Rophe,"** which means **"the Lord your health."**

Actually, it is better to have health than healing.
It is better to not get sick at all, isn't it? God wants His
people to walk in divine health.

Some years ago, the Lord dealt with me about memorizing His Word, so I memorized the book of Proverbs.
Through that memorization, I learned a principle about
the **life** in God's Word. I was in my early forties when I
first began to memorize, and people tried to tell me that
my memory was going to fail. "After forty years old, your
memory goes downhill all the way!"

Don't accept that idea! You have the mind of Christ,
and His mind does not go downhill after age forty. When
I started memorizing, I could learn about one verse each
day. As I stayed with it, I eventually progressed to learning

132

two or three verses a day. And as time passed, I got to where I could memorize fifteen verses a day. **The life of God's Word** was entering my body and **quickening** my brain cells.

God's Word is like medicine. When you take His Word, you are taking in health. That is why God told His people to harken to His Word. God wants His people to be full of His Own life. You may believe in healing, and that's great, but there is more to it. You must **receive** healing. And you will receive it only by reading and meditating on God's Word. You must continuously feed upon His Words of life, health and healing.

Exodus fifteen says that you will not have the diseases of the world, if you will read and meditate upon His Word. He was saying, "Egypt is full of disease because they are full of idolatry. But you won't have their diseases if you will harken to My Words, because **I am the Lord your health! I am your Jehovah Rophe."**

Before this time, there were other healings. Once Abraham lied to a king about his wife, and said, "She's my sister." He was afraid the king of Egypt would kill him and keep Sarah for himself. When the king heard that Sarah was Abraham's sister, naturally he thought nothing of making her part of his harem. (It doesn't pay to lie.)

What happened? The wombs of all the women in his harem were made fruitless; none of them could have children. The Lord waited until the Egyptian king returned Sarah to Abraham before He would heal those women.

Then God entered into a covenant name with Moses, as **Jehovah Rophe.** Moses lived on God's Word, and he believed this statute.

133

And Moses was an hundred and twenty years old when he died: his eye was not dim, nor his natural force abated. (Deuteronomy 34:7)

Why?

Moses fed on God's Word! It was Spirit and life to him because he believed it, and acted on it. Moses trusted in **Jehovah Rophe.** God's life and health was a personal revelation to him, and he received it for himself.

Jehovah Rophe wants to be personal to you, also. He wants to heal you and make you whole!

People have said to me, "The God of the Old Testament is so harsh! He's a God of judgment. The God of the New Testament is a God of mercy."

That is not true. He's the same God.

Jesus Christ the same yesterday, and today, and forever. (Hebrews 13:8)

Every good gift and every perfect gift is from above, and cometh down from the Father of lights, with whom is no variableness, neither shadow of turning. (James 1:17)

God never switched personalities in between Old and New Testament times. He gave us a better covenant, but He is the same! There is **much** scripture about healing in the Old Testament. King David saw God as **Jehovah Rophe.**

1 Bless the LORD, O my soul: and all that is within me, bless his holy name.

2 Bless the LORD, O my soul, and forget not all his benefits:

*3 Who forgiveth all thine iniquities; who heal-
eth all thy diseases.* (Psalm 103:1-3)

Many men in the Old Testament experienced God's
healing power. When Hezekiah thought that he was about
to die, God performed a miracle. The prophet Isaiah had
told Hezekiah, "Set your household in order; you're
going to die."

Then Hezekiah turned his face and cried out, "Oh
God, I don't want to die! I don't have any children, and
there's no one who will take my place."

He prayed, and Isaiah came back and said, "God is
going to add fifteen years to your life."

Hezekiah lived, and had a son whose name was Manasseh. God is a merciful God Who heals His people!

Numbers twelve describes how Moses not only received health for himself, but for others as well. Healing
is not just for you. It is for you to bring forth in others!
Jesus said we are to lay our hands upon the sick, and they
would recover.

When I first started praying for the sick, the devil
said, "If you lay hands on them, they'll die."

One night a Mennonite woman called and asked for
my husband to pray for her husband, after he'd had a heart
attack. My husband was not home, and I was sick with the
flu. I'd been claiming healing for it, but instead, it got
worse.

When the woman asked me to pray, I agreed, even
though my head was spinning. On the way to her house I
murmured, and murmured, "I can't believe for healing
for myself, and here You have me pray for some Mennon-

ite man with a heart attack. He doesn't even believe in healing. I'm supposed to go pray a great prayer of faith, and I can't get well myself!"

When I finally arried, I thought, "If I go in with this attitude and lay hands on that man, he'll die for certain."

I repented of my attitude, and the Lord said sweetly, "Marilyn, you're not going to heal him, I'm going to heal him."

Inside his home, he had passed out on the divan. His wife and I read scriptures and prayed together for him.

We went to the kitchen to go over some scriptures. I wanted to encourage her faith. All of a sudden, he was calling from the living room. We rushed in, and there he was, sitting up, saying, "The terrible pain is gone! I feel fine!"

His wife introduced us, and eventually they began attending church. Later, he became a deacon.

Moses practiced healing; see the book of Numbers. When he married an Ethiopian woman, his sister Miriam, became furious. There was heavy criticism. You might say, "He shouldn't have married her."

I won't discuss whether he should or should not have married her. When others blow it, we're not to be their judge, are we? God knows much more about His children then we know about them. He doesn't need our help in dealing with them. We're not the parents. We are the brothers and sisters.

Moses received the heaviest accusations from Miriam, but his brother Aaron ended up being involved, too. Miriam was the older sister who had sent Moses down the river as a baby, swaddled in a tiny ark. She watched over him in Pharaoh's household, and arranged for his mother to be his wet nurse. She saw him grow up. Miriam knew about his flight from Egypt and his return. As his sister, she was probably very proud of him.

Moses' first wife had left him, and when she did, Miriam had probably stepped in and taken the "hospitality role" as wife. I think she liked being a queen bee.

When Moses married the Ethiopian woman who would take over the duties that Miriam so loved, she got angry! When Miriam started murmuring, she got over into the devil's territory.

9 And the anger of the LORD was kindled against them; and he departed.

10 And the cloud departed from off the tabernacle; and behold Miriam became leprous, white as snow: and Aaron looked upon Miriam, and behold, she was leprous.

11 And Aaron said unto Moses, Alas, my lord, I beseech thee, lay not the sin upon us, wherein we have done foolishly, and wherein we have sinned.

12 Let her not be as one dead, of whom the flesh is half consumed when he cometh out of his mother's womb.

13 And Moses cried unto the LORD, saying, Heal her now, O God, I beseech thee. (Numbers 12:9-13)

How did Moses know that he could pray for her healing?

He had met **Jehovah Rophe!** Notice who prayed for Miriam. It was the one against whom she had murmured. When people speak against you, pray for them and bless them.

That had to be embarrassing for Miriam. She had been the queen bee. She led the women in a dance unto the Lord after crossing the Red Sea. Then she murmured and got leprosy, and everyone knew why. Here is how the Lord answered Moses' prayer.

14 And the LORD said unto Moses, If her father had but spit in her face, should she not be ashamed seven days? let her be shut out from the camp seven days, and after that let her be received in again.

15 And Miriam was shut out from the camp seven days: and the people journeyed not till Miriam was brought in again. (Numbers 12:14-15)

The attitude of Jesus Christ says, "I don't care whether you murmured, I am not moved by circumstances, I am moved by love. I love you, and forgive you." That was the attitude which Moses had for Miriam, and she had to go to him for forgiveness. I'm sure, after spending seven days out of the camp, with leprosy, she never murmured again!

But she was healed. Faith works by love. Moses' faith to ask for healing was motivated by love.

God wants to heal all conditions--physical, spiritual, mental and emotional.

*Return, ye backsliding children, and I will heal
your backslidings.* (Jeremiah 3:22)

Jesus came to heal those with emotional wounds--the
broken hearted, and the bruised. He came to heal people
from backsliding and sin. He came to heal them from
physical afflictions. **Jehovah Rophe is health in every
area of life!**

Jesus quoted Isaiah 61:1-2 in Luke 4:18-19.

*18 The Spirit of the Lord is upon me because he
hath anointed me to preach the gospel to the poor;
he hath sent me to heal the broken hearted, to
preach deliverance to the captives, and recovering
of sight to the blind, to set at liberty them that are
bruised,*

19 To preach the acceptable year of the Lord.

In Isaiah 53, the prophet said that Jesus...

*3 ...is despised and rejected of men; a man of
sorrows, and acquainted with grief...*

*4 Surely he hath borne our griefs, and carried
our sorrows....* (Isaiah 53:3-4)

We not only need to be healed of physical affliction,
but grief and sorrow are needs which also must be healed.
Don't carry grief. Jesus wants you to cast cares upon Him.
Jehovah Rophe wants His people to be free of every
affliction.

When my father died, my mother had a very difficult
time. She grieved for a long time, feeling that there was
no point in continuing with life. She felt that she was no
longer needed. We children tried comforting her, but
nothing seemed to help.

Finally, one day the Lord showed me something that could help.

He said, "She is carrying that grief by herself. Those emotional wounds will cause people to crack under the pressure." So I called her up and asked her,

"Mother, did Jesus take your sins?"

"You know that He did," she said.

I said, "He really carried your sins? You let Him carry them?"

"Yes!" she said.

"Did Jesus come to heal you? Did He take your sickness?" I asked her.

"You know that He did." she responded.

"Mother," I asked, "did Jesus carry your griefs and sorrows?" She stopped and I continued,

"If He carried them, why are you carrying them? If you do not cast that sorrow upon Him, you will die prematurely. I need you. Wally and the Happy Church all need you. The ministry needs you. Cast the grief and sorrow of father's death upon Jesus and let Him carry it."

And from that day on, she no longer tried to carry her sorrows by herself. She gave them over to Jesus.

God has a special medicine cabinet for all kinds of sicknesses. He went to great lengths to provide ways for your healing. He uses prayer cloths, laying on of hands, anointing with oil, and the prayer of faith. Provision for healing takes many different directions!

If you are hurting in the soul area (mind and emotions), **Jehovah Rophe has given you a provision.** Jeremiah asked,

Is there no balm in Gilead; is there no physician there? why then is not the health of the daughter of my people recovered? (Jeremiah 8:22)

There is a song that says, "There is a balm in Gilead that heals the sin-sick soul; there is a balm in Gilead that makes the wounded whole." Jeremiah was asking, isn't there a balm to heal the soul-sick people?

I asked the Lord, "What is the balm that heals sickness of the soul?"

"Look up the word Gilead," He spoke within my spirit. Gilead means "praise." What happens when you praise the Lord?

You bring **Jehovah Rophe** on the scene. You bring in healing!

Have you ever gone into a service feeling down? Soon you begin worshipping and praising the Lord, clapping your hands and singing.

What happened?

You received **healing!**

People who abide in praise, abide in the Lord! They live in health.

Don't get involved in self pity, and all the other garbage that the world is into. You don't have to take the "diseases of the Egyptians." You only need to receive the health of **Jehovah Rophe.**

Jesus was bruised in your place. He came to set you at liberty. When he was hanging there upon the cross, soldiers tried to give him a sponge soaked in myrrh, but Jesus refused to drink it. He refused to drink, because myrrh is a pain-deadener. Jesus carried all of your anxieties, fears, and rejection. He carried all your physical afflictions. They're **not yours** anymore. Why are you carrying them? Why would you carry something, when Jesus took it to the utmost for you? He refused the myrrh. Song of Solomon 1:13 says,

A bundle of myrrh is my well-beloved unto me;
he shall lie all night betwixt my breasts. (Song of Solomon 1:13)

Myrrh smells good, and people use it in many ways. They put it in their clothes, in sacrifices, in incense and oil. It could be crushed into powder, or remain in twigs. This scripture is about Jesus. He is not just a pinch of dried myrrh, or a little drop of oil. He is a whole bundle of myrrh. He has a stick of myrrh for every heartache and heartbreak which you ever encounter. When you allow Jesus to heal wounds in your soul area, not just the physical area, you will really begin to smell victorious! You'll start smelling sweet, like Him.

When the Israelites left Egypt, they ate lamb with bitter herbs. We'll encounter bitter circumstances at times, but if we'll mix them with the Lamb of God, He will bring healing.

The three Hebrew children were thrown in Nebuchadnezzar's furnace for not bowing to the idol, and when they came out, they didn't even **smell** like smoke!

Why?

They were in the fire with Jesus. They did not want to come out, away from Him, and I don't blame them!

Perhaps you have come out of some negative experiences which have wounded you, and you smell like

142

smoke. You still talk and complain about them, and they still show.

Come to Jesus, and cast that wound and hurt upon Him. Let Him remove that smoky smell, and make you smell like myrrh, like Himself, **Jehovah Rophe!**

Jesus is your Jehovah Rophe. He has healing for you. He has healing from sin, backsliding, physical ailments, heart wounds, rejection--everything.

Jehovah Rophe - No matter what sort of affliction may try to attach to you, you can bring forth the healing of **Jehovah Rophe!** He never changes. He is the same today as He was when the children of Israel knew Him as **the Lord our health.** He has wonderful healing for you, throughout the entire Bible. Have you received Him as **"The Lord My Health?"**

For I will restore health unto thee, and I will heal thee of thy wounds, saith the LORD. (Jeremiah 30:17)

Moreover the light of the moon shall be as the light of the sun, and the light of the sun shall be sevenfold, as the light of seven days, in the day that the LORD bindeth up the breach of his people, and healeth the stroke of their wound. (Isaiah 30:26)

And Jesus went about all Galilee, teaching in their synagogues, and preaching the gospel of the kingdom, and healing all manner of sickness and all manner of disease among the people. (Matthew 4:23)

Whosoever drinketh of this water shall thirst again:

But whosoever drinketh of the water that I shall give him shall never thirst; but the water that I shall give him shall be in him a well of water springing up into everlasting life. (John 4:13b-14)

And the Spirit and the bride say, Come. And let him that heareth say, Come. And let him that is athirst come. And whosoever will, let him take the water of life freely. (Revelation 22:17)

Chapter 9

JEHOVAH SHALOM

The image of God's peace within us is one of the most beautiful images that God has put within us. In this busy world, peace may seem hard to come by. It doesn't have to be, when you know Jehovah Shalom. At times, the word **peace** is translated as "whole," or "well," and that should be no surprise. Peace is the one quality which the world cannot buy, for all of its money.

There is a saying, "No God, no peace--Know God, know peace," and that is true. Ever eluding the world in all of their activity, how wonderful it is that we, the children of **Jehovah Shalom,** have exactly what the world is looking for--peace.

The Word of God says the Lord gives us an abundance of peace. In this study of Jehovah Shalom, I think you will see a whole new concept of who Jesus is in your life and heart.

The first revelation of Jehovah Shalom is found in Judges six. It is about a young man who seemed to have less peace than anyone. His name was Gideon. First, look at some of the history. Two hundred years previously, Jehovah had revealed Himself as the One Who sanctified His people. Since that time, Joshua had passed away, and no central government existed between the tribes, which were scattered about the land. Israel had forgotten about Jehovah, their God.

They turned instead to the gods of the idolatrous people with the land. The Bible says that every man was only doing what seemed right in his own eyes. As a result of their sinfulness, the Israelites were in the place of great defeat.

The "numberless" troops of Midianites had overcome Israel, using their secret weapon, the camel. The Israelites had never seen men on camels, attacking with swords. They came in and took over, burning the children of Israel's crops as they went along.

Why did this happen?

It happened because the Israelites were backslidden from God. They had forgotten the peace which was to accompany their heritage as a chosen nation.

You remember that Gideon was a man with a tremendous inferiority complex--without much going for himself at the time. The Lord wanted him to battle the Midianites.But of course, he thought that couldn't possibly be--even though the Lord told him, "Surely I will be with you, and you shall smite the Midianites as one man."'

Jesus inside of you is what gives you strength! So many times, it's easy to get uptight about the way things look. When David fought Goliath, he was brave and bold, even though Goliath was probably towering eight feet over his head. David could have peace because he considered how big God was, and not his own size.

When Gideon got upset about the sacrifice being burned up, saying that he had seen God and was going to die, the Lord spoke to him very beautifully.

23 And the LORD said unto him, Peace be unto thee; fear not: thou shalt not die.

24 Then Gideon built an altar there unto the LORD, and called it Jehovah Shalom: unto this day it is yet in Ophrah of the Abiezrites. (Judges 6:23-24)

God gave Gideon peace within his spirit before he ever won the battle. What God does! Peace does not come because of outward situations. Peace comes because of Him Who is inside you. God is greater than anything you may encounter in this world. God wants you to make **Him** your peace, not the circumstances. Philippians 4:6-7 tells you how peace works.

6 Be careful for nothing; but in everything by prayer and supplication with thanksgiving let your requests be made known unto God.

7 And the peace of God which passeth all understanding, shall keep your hearts and minds through Christ Jesus. (Philippians 4:6-7)

God is saying, "Don't get all uptight about anything. If you need something, pray, ask for it, and thank Me for it."

It is important to thank God after He answers your prayer! When you pray and thank Him that His provision has been made, let His peace **keep** you.

Consider the word **Shalom.** When you visit Israel, they say to you, "Shalom, shalom!" I asked someone why they say it twice. It is because they want you to have peace in the inner man and peace in the outer man. Shalom, meaning "whole," shows you that, when God's peace reigns in your heart, you are whole!

It can also mean "full." You are **full,** lacking nothing in Christ Jesus!

Another interesting definition for the word shalom is "to pay or render." Peace is God's **payment** which says, "I don't have to worry about the future, because I know that His Word has paid for my provision."

A final meaning for shalom is so beautiful that I won't expand on it. This word says "peace," better than any-- **perfect.**

The word shalom is very important. It is used 170 times throughout the Bible, translated simply "peace." The prophet Isaiah prophesied that Jesus would come as the prince of Peace (Isaiah 9:6). Jerusalem, Jesus' city, means "the city of peace," or "the possession of peace."

You can recall the five different offerings, one of which is a "peace offering." It was not an offering which would cause them to **obtain** peace. It was a celebration of already having it. **Jehovah Shalom** came to bring peace to His people.

For I know the thoughts that I think toward you, saith the LORD, thoughts of peace, and not evil. (Jeremiah 29:11)

God said, "I have peace for you!" God does not want you to be confused and torn up. He wants you to be single-

148

minded and full of His peace.

Some have thought, "God gives me many bad things so that I'll mature and be purified."

That is **not** what God's Word says! The Bible says clearly in James 1:17 that every **good** thing comes from God!

O that thou hadst harkened to my commandments! then had thy peace been as a river and thy righteousness as the waves of the sea. (Isaiah 48:18)

When you obey the Word of God, you will have peace that flows from you like a river, touching other people. Even though you may not see victory, or feel that a victory is near, you have to let God's peace keep you!

David said in Psalm 29:11 that it is your heritage to have peace. The Lord will bless His people with peace. Peace is your blessing, and it is for every possible situation.

How do I know that? The word "blessing" is always used in the plural form. God cannot give you a singular blessing. He is a God of many blessings--**El Shaddai!**

He wants you to have peace that is so abundant that it resembles a great flowing river!

For thus saith the LORD, behold, I will extend peace to her like a river. (Isaiah 66:12)

Recall that Gideon had only three hundred men to fight the enormous Midianite army. But even **they** were speaking victory! One night, God told him, "If you're **still** afraid, and you're not full of my peace, go and listen inside the enemy camp."

149

He wasn't feeling very peaceful, so he slipped in and listened outside one of the Midianite tents.

13 And when Gideon was come, behold, there was a man that told a dream unto his fellow, and said, Behold, I dreamed a dream and, lo, a cake of barley bread tumbled into the host of Midian, and came unto a tent, and smote it that it fell, and overturned it, that the tent lay along.

14 And His fellow answered and said, This is nothing else save the sword of Gideon the son of Joash, a man of Israel: for into his hand hath God delivered Midian, and all the host. (Judges 7:13-14)

Gideon heard a man say, "I dreamed that a huge barley loaf rolled down the mountain and knocked down the tent." The other was heard to say, "Gideon will slay us and win."

Gideon heard the **enemy** say that, even though there were only three hundred men to fight. Naturally, they did win the battle. God had said that they would, and His Word is never void of the promised results. It always works--that should give you peace.

After the battle, Gideon's relatives asked him, "Why didn't you call us earlier so that we could have been in the battle, too? You just wanted to be a big cheese!"

But Gideon kept peace with his relatives, even through all of that. He had a revelation of **Jehovah Shalom.** When you can keep peace with your unsaved relatives, that is really something. It's a witness to them, and a way to let Jesus' light shine out.

Why?

You have peace, and that is something that they want!

When Gideon's relatives griped at him, he could have said, "If you're so smart, why didn't you come out and fight with us? I just did what God led me to do. Are you arguing with His leadings in my life? We won; isn't that what counts?"

Instead, he said, "What would we have done without you? You're part of this. After all, you came and cleaned up the whole Midianite army. God led you here, so who are we, in comparison to you?"

That is tact, flowing out of a man who is full of **Jehovah's peace.**

Gideon's relatives shut up, and everything between them was peaceful. When you are full of peace, you'll have peaceful relationships. Contention takes two people. Peace takes only one. When you let Jesus' peace, love and joy flow out, there can't be any strife.

There is another quality to having peace like a river. You won't run short of a supply! Jesus was promised to be the Prince of Peace in Isaiah 9:6. Luke 1:78 says, *"Through the tender mercy of our God; whereby the dayspring from on high hath visited us,"* and Zechariah prophesied that this Dayspring would guide our feet into the way of peace.

What is to be upon our feet? Ephesians 6:15 says that we are to have our *"feet shod with the preparation of the gospel of peace."* God's Word made flesh, Jesus, is our **Jehovah Shalom.** He'll give you wholeness, completeness, and peace.

One definition of peace is "living life at its best." It doesn't just mean "not having a fight." The Greek word for peace is **eirene,** and it means exactly, **to live life at its best!**

What is your life like now? Is it full of **Jehovah Shalom's peace?**

At Jesus' birth, a multitude of heavenly hosts sang this song together.

Glory to God in the highest and on earth peace, good will toward men. (Luke 2:14)

Peace Himself came and dwelt in the body of a man, was crucified, and rose from the dead, so that **you** could have His peace! Jesus told many people whom He healed, "Go in peace."

He knew what he was talking about. When Jesus wept over Jerusalem in Luke 19:42, He cried,

...If thou hadst known, even thou, at least in this thy day, the things which belong unto thy peace! (Luke 19:42)

The people of God are to have, and leave, a heritage of peace. What were His words to the disciples after His resurrection? "Peace be unto you."

Paul said that Jesus *...came and preached peace to you which were afar off, and to them that were nigh* (Ephesians 2:17). Jesus has already accomplished peace for you, because He is the Prince of Peace. Jesus gave us peace with God through Himself, because we were reconciled to God through His death. The Bible says Jesus has reconciled all things, both in heaven and in earth, through His blood. His blood cries out, "Peace, peace."

Hebrews 12:24 says that Jesus' blood speaks better things than Abel's blood which cried out to God in the book of Genesis. What does Jesus' blood say? It says, **"Peace."**

Jesus paid a dear and precious price for you to have peace. How dare you not walk, live in, and claim it?

And let the peace of God rule in your hearts. (Colossians 3:15)

You have to decide which way you will yield your emotions. Are you yielding them to the peace of God, or to worry? Let the peace of God rule and reign. You are not to worry or be anxious, because **Jehovah Shalom** gave you peace. He wants you to know that He is in control.

Thou wilt keep him in perfect peace, whose mind is stayed on thee: because he trusteth in thee. (Isaiah 26:3)

Romans 8:6 says, *"...to be spiritually minded is life and peace."* When you are upset, you aren't being spiritually minded. You don't have your mind stayed (or fastened) where it should be. Fasten your mind upon the Lord!

Don't let your mind get restless and take over. The root word for **wicked** means "restless." Don't live in that heritage of being carnally minded. Take your heritage of peace from **Jehovah Shalom.**

Isaiah said the work of righteousness is peace. (Isaiah 32:17) The effect of righteousness is quietness and assurance forever. That doesn't mean you speak softly and hardly ever talk. It means you have a **quiet** spirit that dominates your soul with God's peace!

When Melchisedek appeared to Abraham, Abraham called him the king of righteousness and the king of peace. **First,** he was righteousness. When you took Jesus as your Lord and Savior, you became the righteousness of God in Him, according to His Word. Jesus is made unto you righteousness. Peace accompanies that.

When Jesus clothed you with His Own right-standing with God, He gave you peace with God--something you never had before! And now that you have peace with God, you can have peace in every situation!

It brings glory to God when you walk in peace on this earth. When you walk in His peace and welfare, what a reputation it gives Him. Restless, uptight, upset Christians do not bring any glory whatsoever to God.

Everywhere in the New Testament, peace is spoken of as an attribute of God the Father, and from the Lord Jesus Christ. Don't take it for granted--they didn't.

You really don't have to ask for peace. Jesus already gave it to you, and it is always available for you. But you do need to claim what is yours. It's not a promise, it's a fact! Jesus is inside of you. You took Him as Lord and Savior, so you have His peace. **He is Jehovah Shalom.**

Gideon continued to walk in peace. The people wanted to make him a judge and ruler over them. But he said, "No, I'm not going to rule over you, and neither are my sons. God will rule over you." Gideon had peace in all situations, after he met **Jehovah Shalom.**

The people changed his name from Jerubbaal to Jerubbesheth, which means "God hath put to shame." Did you know that God's peace will put every enemy to shame? Nothing can shake you up when you're walking surrounded in His peace!

Peace ruled in Gideon's life, and it can rule in yours. Are you living life at its best? Do you have peace in all situations? Peace will not leave you. Jesus said that He would **never** leave you nor forsake you. His peace is better than anything which the world could ever offer.

27 Peace I leave with you, my peace I give unto you: not as the world giveth, give I unto you. Let not your heart be troubled, neither let it be afraid,

28 Ye have heard how I said unto you, I go away, and come again unto you. If ye loved me, ye would rejoice,.... (John 14:27-28)

He's coming back soon! Live in His peace. Let it reign and rule in your life. Be spiritually minded. **He is Jehovah Shalom**--and that is something to have peace about.

Jehovah Shalom - You can have peace while everyone and everything around you seems to be falling apart. You can be a river of **peace** whose peace flows upon others. The God of **peace, Jehovah Shalom,** is in you specifically for that reason. He shared His peace with you. He gave you peace with Himself. Now share it with someone else.

3 If ye walk in my statutes, and keep my commandments and do them...

6 ...I will give peace in the land, and ye shall lie down, and none shall make you afraid: and I will rid evil beasts out of the land, neither shall the sword go through your land. (Leviticus 26:3,6)

24 The LORD bless thee, and keep thee:

25 The LORD make his face shine upon thee, and be gracious unto thee:

26 The LORD lift up his countenance upon thee, and give thee peace. (Numbers 6:24-26)

28 Come unto me, all ye that labour and are heavy laden, and I will give you rest.

29 Take my yoke upon you, and learn of me; for I am meek and lowly in heart: and ye shall find rest unto your souls. Matthew 11:28-29)

And the peace of God, which passeth all understanding, shall keep your hearts and minds through Christ Jesus. (Philippians 4:7)

Peace I leave with you, my peace I give unto you: not as the world giveth, give I unto you. Let not your heart be troubled, neither let it be afraid. (John 14:27)

Chapter 10

JEHOVAH TSIDKENU

Jehovah Tsidkenu means **"Jehovah our Righteousness,"** and it appears in a prophecy by Jeremiah.

5 Behold, the days come, saith the Lord, that I will raise unto David a righteous Branch and a King shall reign and prosper, and shall execute judgment and justice in the earth.

6 In his days Judah shall be saved, and Israel shall dwell safely: and this is his name whereby he shall be called, **THE LORD OUR RIGHTEOUSNESS.** (Jeremiah 23:5-6)

Even though we know Jesus is the Righteous Branch, and we know we are in His Body, we often see ourselves as still being unrighteous, and full of sin. All of us have felt that way, but if you're speaking words like that out of your mouth, then you are defeating yourself, because they are unscriptural words.

I've heard of people who say things like, "Oh no! My righteousness is as filthy rags--Isaiah 64:6!" In your past, your righteousness was as filthy rags, and it would never have sufficed to give you a relationship with God. But when you came to Jesus, that all changed. The New Testament says you are the righteousness of God in Christ Jesus. When you begin to see your rightstanding with God, your entire life will be changed. You'll begin to move into a new area of faith, and your whole life will flow in righteousness as it never has before.

Basically, righteousness means "the quality of being right." It shows the picture of a man trusting in God, and becoming the righteousness of God. When Jeremiah uttered the prophecy about a Righteous Branch, the kingdom of Judah was in a terrible state of sinfulness.

More than one hundred years before this period of time, the ten tribes of the kingdom of Israel had been taken into captivity, never to return. But Judah, the southern kingdom, hadn't learned anything from this lesson. In fact, they became even worse than the tribes which had been in the north.

Jeremiah's ministry began during the reign of a very good king named Josiah. Over the years, there had been both good kings and bad kings. Israel had experienced reformation after counter-reformation. This shows the nation's instability in every area of life.

Judah was on a downhill trend. So when Josiah came on the scene, it was exciting to see the wonderful reforms which he made--especially for those people who could compare it to the time when Manasseh ruled. For Manasseh had been a vicious, cruel king who reigned for fifty-five years, and caused nothing but trouble and terror. Historians say he was the king who killed the prophet Isaiah by sawing him in two.

Finally, Manasseh repented and turned around, but he reigned only his last two years as a Godly man. That isn't long enough to do much for a country. His son Ammon came to the throne, and raised up all the idols his father pulled down. He reigned for only two years, for his own servants murdered him. For the Israelites, to get a king like Josiah was an answered prayer.

Unfortunately, King Josiah came to an untimely death, and the whole scene began to change again. The land was full of oppression, violence, political intrigue and unrest. God warned the Israelites and sent messages through the prophets.

...until the wrath of the LORD arose against his people, till there was no remedy. (2nd Chronicles 36:16b)

God was saying, *I have had enough!*

The beautiful prophet, Jeremiah, asked God to give him eyes that would weep for his nation. He wept over the sins of Israel. He wasn't a smart aleck who went around telling them how bad they were. He identified with them in their sin. He was a broken man, wanting to prompt brokenness in the hearts and lives of the people.

In all of this darkness throughout the nation, Jeremiah prophesied God's Word (Jeremiah 23:5-6). When things were at their very darkest, Jeremiah stood up and said, "This King will be righteousness."

Instead of seeking the healing touch of Jehovah Rophe, the Israelites rejected his healing power which would heal their sins and their bodies. When Jehovah Nissi could have gone before them in victory and been their Banner, they did their own thing. They rejected Him. As a result, at every turn, they were defeated. They would not let God be Jehovah M'Kaddesh, the One Who sanctifies. To set themselves apart was the last thing they had in mind. So how could God become their righteousness? It seemed impossible.

The Hebrew word **tsedek** originally meant "to be stiff or straight." It can mean "a full weight or measure" toward God in the spiritual sense. One time, God told the people, "When you sacrifice, don't just give Me animals. A true sacrifice is a broken spirit, and a contrite heart." (Psalm 51:16-17) Job himself said, "How shall a man be righteous with God? These sacrifices are not enough."

Who is righteous? Jehovah is perfect righteousness. The psalmist said there was none to compare to Him. He is righteous and right!

Psalm 119 speaks of **Jehovah Tsidkenu.**

142 Thy righteousness is an everlasting righteousness, and thy law is the truth.

144 The righteousness of thy testimonies is everlasting: give me understanding, and I shall live. (Psalm 119:142, 144)

God is saying, "I am righteous, and children are like their parents. If you are going to be my children, you will be righteous, also."

Israel was so tangled up with their sacrifices, and the fact that Abraham was their father, that they never thought

160

about God making them righteous. They thought their acts could be their righteousness.

If you don't smoke, drink, curse, murder nor commit adultery, does that put you in right-standing with God? Isaiah 64:6 says that your own righteousness is disgusting to God. It is like filthy rags.

The apostle Paul had been extremely proud of his merit. He was a Pharisee of the Pharisees. He was from the tribe of Benjamin, and had studied at the feet of Gamaliel, a doctor of the law. But after his conversion, Paul said that he had been the **worst** of all sinners.

The heart is deceitful above all things, and desperately wicked: who can know it? (Jeremiah 17:9)

Behold, I was shapen in iniquity; and in sin did my mother conceive me. (Psalm 51:5)

How then can man be justified (righteous) with God? or how can he be clean that is born of a woman? (Job 25:4)

You may do every imaginable thing correctly, but there is still sin in your spirit, unless you have met **Jehovah Tsidkenu--the Lord Who will be your righteousness.** No person could ever redeem you.

None of them can by any means redeem his brother, nor give to God a ransom for him. (Psalm 49:7)

Only the Righteous Servant, found in Isaiah 53 could pay for your ransom. He is the Holy One of Israel. He is the Branch of David. He is your Righteousness, in person.

What does that mean to you? Peter called Jesus the "Holy One," and the "Righteous One." The psalmist said,

161

"There will be one who will cover all their sins."

I will greatly rejoice in the LORD (Jehovah), my soul shall be joyful in my God; for he hath clothed me with the garments of salvation, he hath covered me with the robe or righteousness, as a bridegroom decketh himself with ornaments, and as a bride adorneth herself with her jewels. (Isaiah 61:10)

He was saying, "There is a Messiah coming Who will be righteous Himself. He will make me righteous by clothing me in His Own." **He'll exchange my filthy rags for a beautiful robe of righteousness.**

Are you in Jesus Christ, as a part of His Own Body, because you've confessed Him with your mouth, and believed upon Him in your heart?

17 Therefore if any man be in Christ, he is a new creature: old things are passed away; behold, all things are become new.

18 And all things are of God who hath reconciled us to himself by Jesus Christ, and hath given to us the ministry of reconciliation.

21 For he hath made him to be sin for us, who knew no sin; that we might be made the righteousness of God in him. (2nd Corinthians 5:17-18,21)

You are a new creature in Christ Jesus, and you are made His righteousness. Not only do you have the Righteous Branch and Jehovah Tsidkenu, but also He made you yourself into **Tsidkenu!** That new creature is not an old mattress that's been renovated. You are a brand new species. You are a creation that has never before existed. Jesus remade you into the righteousness of God in Him, to fulfill a part that no one else can fulfill.

Sometimes, just saying, "I am the righteousness of God!" makes me feel better and act better. When you start saying who you are, you start acting like who you are. A lot of people want it the other way around. Realize what Jesus Christ has created you to be. Until you can see that image, you will be a defeated Christian.

Ephesians 4:24,25 says that you are to actively receive Jesus' righteousness.

24 And that ye put on the new man, which after God is created in righteousness and true holiness.

25 Wherefore putting away lying, speak every man truth with his neighbor: for we are members one of another. (Ephesians 4:24-25)

You must decide to put on the new man who is clothed in Jesus' righteousness. God is not going to force you to act like a new creature. Every day, say, "I am a new man. I'm a new creation. I'm the righteousness of God in Christ Jesus."

It is really true that our righteousness is as filthy rags, as Isaiah said. It's your past, and my past, but Jesus swapped with us. He took our sins and destroyed the powers of darkness. Then He gave us His righteousness.

No wonder every promise in the Bible is ours! No wonder He saw fit to renew our minds in it! There is no condemnation to those who are in Christ Jesus, because they are clothed in His right-standing with God.

Say to yourself, "I am partaking of the Lord's divine nature, which has never sinned. I am partaking of His righteousness.''

God no longer looks at you through your sins. Now He looks at you through the righteousness of His Son, Jesus Christ,

> *Confess your faults one to another, and pray one for another, that ye may be healed. The effectual fervent prayer of a **righteous** man availeth much.* (James 5:16)

Who is a righteous man?

A righteous man is one who is born again into Jesus' righteousness. **That righteous man's prayers avail much!**

Jesus' righteousness will cause your prayers to avail much. His righteousness covers your spirit, your personality, your mind, and your emotions. You can command your body and soul to shape up and get in line with God's Word. Tell them, "You start acting like your Father, **Jehovah Tsidkenu!**"

You might ask, "What about my past? What about the bad things that I repented of?"

The Bible says your old life is dead. Your past is dead, so leave it alone.

Paul had a bold confession of faith.

> *I am crucified with Christ: nevertheless I live; yet not I, but Christ liveth in me: and the life which I now live in the flesh I live by the faith of the Son of God, who loved me, and gave himself for me.* (Galatians 2:20)

Jesus is made unto you wisdom **and** righteousness. A lot of people claim His wisdom, but they don't say anything about His righteousness. You need both.

But he that is joined unto the Lord is one spirit. (1st Corinthians 6:17)

It is an amazing miracle to be able to partake of the very Spirit of Jesus. It is His Spirit, the Holy Spirit, Who causes you to be His righteousness, and therefore causes you to overcome death and the grave itself!

O death, where is thy sting? O grave, where is thy victory? (1st Corinthians 15:55)

Sometimes it's easy to get glum. Maybe you have fought with your spouse, or screamed at the children. Perhaps something dreadful has gone wrong at work, or you just plain had a bad day. During those times, If someone came up and said, "You're the righteousness of God," you would say, "I'm anything but the righteousness of God!"

But when we repent of attitude sins, and sins against others, what happens? Does He take us back, and are we still righteous? First John 1:9 says, when we confess our sins, the Lord is faithful and just to forgive us, and to **cleanse** us from all unrighteousness! Repentance brings cleansing.

But even better than always repenting and being cleansed, is what Paul said in Corinthians.

Awake to righteousness, and sin not; for some have not the knowledge of God: I speak this to your shame. (1st Corinthians 15:34)

Awake to who you are! Put on that image, and let it shine out of you and reach others for the kingdom of God.

165

You have been born anew into God's righteousness. When you see yourself as a sinner, you'll keep entering areas of sin. When you see yourself as righteous and complete in Jesus Christ, you'll avoid those areas. You'll resist the enemy's attacks.

Manasseh was one of the worst men in the Bible. He was a real thug! For 53 years, he reigned over Israel, and did every evil thing that he could do. He built idols and got Israel involved in Baal worship again. He set up horoscopes and astrology.

He made a graven image and put it in the holy of holies, where God's presence had been seen. When people opposed him, he turned lions against them. When the prophet Isaiah opposed Manasseh, of course, Isaiah was put to death. Manasseh even passed his own children through fire as a sacrifice to an idol. What a wicked king!

God dealt with Manasseh in a severe way. He sent the Assyrian army against him. Manasseh was taken captive and put into a Babylonian prison, where he was very mistreated. The Bible says that while Manasseh was in affliction, he prayed and repented before God.

Then God cleansed him of his sins, and sent him back to his throne in Jerusalem. The last two years of Manasseh's reign were tremendous. He took down all of the idols, cleaned out the temple, and called the nation to worship Jehovah God.

Manasseh was once a very wicked man, but what is he today? He is the righteousness of God in Christ Jesus. I think, when he arrived in heaven, the first person he looked up was Isaiah. He probably said, "Hey, Isaiah, I'm the man who cut you in half."

Isaiah probably said, "Don't worry about it, Manasseh. You repented of your sin, and for me, it was just a shortcut to glory."

Have you cut any prophets in half lately? Have you killed any Christians, like the apostle Paul once did? When those men repented, they became God's righteousness, because God cleansed them.

The Bible says, *"Let this mind be in you, which was also in Christ Jesus."* (Philippians 2:5)

What mind is that?

It is His righteous mind! You can think right thoughts and do right acts, because of Jesus in you.

When the prodigal son ran off, he spent all that was his. When he returned to his father, one of the things his father gave him was a robe. He said, "Give my son the best robe." The best is always the robe that the father wore.

That son, who had been living with pigs and had wasted his father's provision for him, was given the best robe. When you came to Jesus, the Father gave you the best robe, the one that He wears, **righteousness.** He took prodigals, those who had spent all He had given them, and had ripped up their privileges, and He **cleansed them and clothed them in His righteousness.** That's what **you** are clothed in, and it came out of heaven's wardrobe.

You will never buy a more expensive robe than the one which the Lord gave you. It was paid for with Jesus' blood. You will never wear a more beautiful, more original creation. It is the righteousness of the Father and Son themselves.

Jesus triumphed over Satan in three areas. In the wilderness, Jesus overcame him, saying, "It is written," and

167

Satan had to obey the Word of God. On the Cross, Jesus stripped Satan of his power, because Jesus overcame sin and took the keys of hell and death. And at your new birth, Jesus won again. He defeated Satan by making you and me--and all of mankind--victors over sin and death.

You are victorious over Satan today, because Jesus gave you His own righteousness, if you've received Him. Don't ever say that you are unrighteous. You are not a poor, lost sinner! You were once, but now you are the righteousness of God. **He is Jehovah Tsidkenu, the Lord YOUR Righteousness.**

Say it! Claim it! A precious price was paid for that robe you are wearing. Don't deny that you have it on.

That righteous robe gives you a prayer power. Pray up a storm, because you have a force and strength to bring tremendous results--His righteousness. **Pray in it, walk in it, live in the beautiful robe which was bought for you by Jehovah Tsidkenu.**

Jehovah Tsidkenu - What a wonderful name this is, revealing the fullness of the measure of our acceptance in the presence of God. How wonderful to have been able to put off the filthy rags of the old man. Now we are dressed in Jesus Himself, by His wonderful Spirit, in righteousness! Have you dressed yourself in the free gift of **Jehovah Tsidkenu--His righteousness?**

17 But God be thanked, that ye were the servants of sin, but ye have obeyed from the heart that form of doctrine which was delivered you.

18 Being then made free from sin, ye became the servants of righteousness. (Romans 6:17-18)

3 For they being ignorant of God's righteousness, and going about to establish their own righteousness, have not submitted themselves unto the righteousness of God.

4 For Christ is the end of the law for righteousness to every one that believeth. (Romans 10:3-4)

But of him are ye in Christ Jesus, who of God is made unto us wisdom, and righteousness, and sanctification, and redemption. (1st Corinthians 1:30)

He shall see of the travail of his soul, and shall be satisfied: by his knowledge shall my righteous servant justify many; for he shall bear their iniquities. (Isaiah 53:11)

Chapter 11

JEHOVAH ROHI

The name **Jehovah Rohi** means **"Jehovah my Shepherd."** The enemy likes to tell Christians they cannot find God's will, or know God's will. Have you ever felt that way? Have you ever heard anyone say, "If I could ever find the will of God...." Some Christians wander through their spiritual walk always searching for His will, and never knowing quite what it is.

Why?

They do not know the Lord as **Jehovah Rohi; Jehovah their Shepherd.**

In Psalm 23, David said, "The Lord is my Shepherd," and he proceeded to give a very personal portrayal of Jehovah Rohi. When you study this name, don't think of Him as "every Christian's Shepherd." **Think of Him as YOUR Shepherd, Who wants you to know His will.**

Personalize the scriptures in this study, and make them your own. Psalm 23 was written by David, the shepherd boy who became Israel's king, and he was a "type" of our Great Shepherd--the Lord Jesus Christ.

The word for **shepherd** has a number of meanings, and you are going to see how they apply to Jesus, and know how He leads and guides you. So don't walk around saying, "I never know the will of God." You **can** know, because He lives inside of you. He wants you to know what His will is for you.

The primary meaning of the word **Rohi** is "to feed." This word was first used when Joseph fed the flock with his brothers, in Genesis 37:2. When the Pharaoh learned that Joseph's family was moving to Egypt, Joseph told him, *47:3 . . . Thy servants are shepherds, both we, and also our fathers. 47:4 . . . thy servants have no pasture for their flocks....* (Genesis 47:3-4). Joseph, and later on, King David, were both great leaders of Israel who started out as shepherds.

Throughout this study on the name **Jehovah Rohi,** you will see how the word **Rohi** relates to **your relationship with the Lord.** Many times, it has to do with feeding.

A second meaning of the word **Rohi** is used to indicate **the relationship between a prince (leader) and his people.** The tribes of Israel said to David,

> *...thou wast he that leddest out and broughtest in Israel: and the LORD said to thee, Thou shalt feed my people Israel, and thou shalt be a captain over Israel.* (2nd Samuel 5:2)

David was to lead his people in a relationship to them as their leader, or director.

Rohi can also signify **the relationship between a priest or prophet and his people.** Jehovah God promised,

>...*I will give you pastors according to mine heart, which shall feed you with knowledge and understanding.* (Jeremiah 3:15)

Jehovah God promised to give you pastors who will feed you with knowledge of the Word. They will explain it to you so that you can understand it. After that, you have a responsibility to apply the Word that you have learned to your own life. If you understand what it says, then you are to **let it become a practical reality in your everyday life.**

The word **Rohi** can be used with regard to folly and judgement. Jehovah Rohi wants to lead you away from folly!

>...*the mouth of fools feedeth on foolishness.* (Proverbs 15:14b)

>an idolater, in his folly, ...*feedeth on ashes.* (Isaiah 44:20)

>Ephraim, full of lies and deceit,...*feedeth on wind....* (Hosea 12:1)

Ezekiel 34:16 says that Jehovah will feed false shepherds with judgement. All of these verses relate to the word Rohi in **feeding.**

A beautiful translation of **Rohi** is that of our "companion," or "friend." This expresses the idea of intimacy and sharing life and food. Jesus is our Great Shepherd, and we are very intimate with Him. The Bible says we are joint heirs with Him (Romans 8:17), we are to share in His life, and be led by Him, identifying completely with Him. Exodus 33:11 spoke of a **Rohi** relationship between the Lord and Moses--*And the Lord spake unto Moses face to face, as a man speaketh unto his friend.*

God wants to be that intimate in His relationship with you. **Jesus is your friend that sticks closer than a brother**--that is your ROHI relationship with Him.

When you see the Lord as your Shepherd, remember all that it involves--He will lead you, feed you, bring judgement, and keep you from folly. He is your close and intimate companion and friend.

The highest aspect of your relationship with the Lord is that Jehovah--this very close One--has redeemed you. He has led you out of sin, and He desires to continue leading you away from sin.

God said to David, "As your Shepherd, I took you out and chose you, David, to feed Jacob this people and Israel his inheritance." Jehovah fed His flock according to the integrity of His heart.. God wants to feed you with goodness, and lead you away from wild grass or oats that would harm you. He is your Shepherd.

The Lord also shows how **you** are to lead, as you take His hand in yours. He is your perfect example.

10 Behold, the Lord GOD will come with strong hand, and his arm shall rule for him: behold, his reward is with him, and his work before him.

11 He shall feed his flock like a shepherd: he shall gather the lambs with his arms, and carry them in his bosom, and shall gently lead those that are with young. (Isaiah 40:10-11)

174

That scripture shows God's strength, but it also shows His tenderness, a part of His image in you. When you are leading others, you are to show both of those qualities. You can discern a false shepherd by being aware of the qualities of a true shepherd.

The true shepherd will seek that which is lost. He will bring again that which was driven away, and bind up that which was broken. He will strengthen that which was sick. God said that He would search out false shepherds and drive them away.

When you see someone come into a church and begin splitting it up, driving people off, he is not a true shepherd. If a person is not strengthening the sick and unhappy, or encouraging them, if he makes them unhappy and causes people to be wounded, rather than supporting them, that is not the spirit of the true shepherd.

If you are acting like that, hurting sheep in the church, if you are tearing at the broken hearted, rather than binding them up, then you are not acting like Jehovah Rohi, your perfect Example.

One time, a man came to my husband and me and said, "There are some things that I don't like in the church. I am a member, but I'm going to withdraw until they get straightened out, because I am a watcher of the sheep." The Bible says that when the wolf comes, the false shepherd runs off!

When there is trouble in a church, the people who run away from it aren't true shepherds. A true shepherd will stay in there, driving the wolves out. The Bible gives you valuable patterns with which to judge yourself. If you will judge yourself accordingly, then you won't have to

175

be judged.

In Genesis 49:24, Jacob called **Jehovah Rohi, "The Mighty God, the Shepherd."**

10 But his bow abode in strength, and the arms of his hands were made strong by the hands of the mighty God of Jacob; (from thence is the shepherd, the stone of Israel:) (Genesis 49:24)

11 He shall feed his flock like a shepherd: . . . and shall gently lead those that are with young. (Isaiah 40:11)

These two descriptions are both combinations of the strength and gentleness of the Lord. There are times when your pastor may need to be very strong. There are also times when he will be very gentle.

Likewise, there are times when Jesus inside of you will be very strong-handed with you. But His strength is always loving! He is a gentle Shepherd, and that is His image in you. Everything that the shepherd is to sheep, Jehovah is toward you.

And I will dwell among the children of Israel. (Exodus 29:45)

The word **dwell** is the Hebrew word **shekinah,** which denotes the glorious presence of God. Jesus in you is greater than he that is in the world, because Jehovah the Shepherd offers the intimacy of His presence. His presence is glorious!

You have the glory of Jehovah living within yourself. When you look at yourself, see His glory. If you've been seeing defeat, you've been looking at the wrong image.

The Lord wants to reveal Himself through you, and He is anything but defeated!

Jehovah Rohi is your Shepherd. He knows you from the inside out.

Thou knowest my downsitting and mine uprising, thou understandest my thoughts afar off. (Psalms 139:2)

He was saying, "You know exactly where I am, and how to take care of me. You are leading and guiding me."

I found some of the most beautiful examples of the Good Shepherd in John 10:11, where Jesus said, "I am the Good Shepherd." The word **good** actually means "appealing." Jesus in you is appealing! One time, my husband said, "Marilyn, if you present Jesus as He really is, He is irresistible." **When you let the image of your Good Shepherd shine through, He'll make YOU irresistible!** That is why Jesus said,

And I, if I be lifted up from the earth, will draw all men unto me. (John 12:32)

People cannot resist the appeal of Jehovah Rohi. Ezekiel said about Jesus,

11 ...Behold, I, even I, will both search my sheep, and seek them out.

12 ...and will deliver them....

14 I will feed them in a good pasture,..

15 ...I will cause them to lie down,,

16 I will seek that which was lost, and bring again that which was driven away, and will

177

bind up that which was broken, and will strengthen that which was sick.... (Ezekiel 34:11,12,14,15,16)

That is exactly what Jesus did for mankind. He came to earth and said, "I am the Good Shepherd. My sheep will know me, because I call them by name. I'll lead them and take care of them. I'll never leave nor forsake them!" Jesus told Peter. "Feed my lambs, feed my sheep." That was the Good Shepherd speaking to the "under-shepherd." Peter reminds us that we had all gone astray like lost sheep--but we've returned to Him Who is the Shepherd and Bishop of our souls!

Sheep can get lost more quickly than any other animal. But when we were astray, Jesus led us back to take care of us.

Jesus is the Shepherd, but He also became the sacrifice lamb, in order to be the Good Shepherd. Sheep that follow the shepherd get acquainted with him according to how much time they spend together.

Jesus called you by your name. You know Him because you recognize His voice, His call. But although a shepherd may not have been a sheep, and not know what they think, it's different with Jesus. He came to earth, and lived as a sheep--He became **the Sacrifice Lamb,** and therefore He knows you intimately.

He came down to earth and showed us mercy. The word for mercy is **chesedeh,** which means **"to climb into someone's skin and look out of his eyes, hear out of his ears and feel what he feels."** Jesus walked in the flesh. He was tempted every way you could possibly be tempted, and He suffered in every way you could suffer.

Why? He climbed into your skin so that He could experience exactly what you'll experience. Then He could give you His mercy! Who could be a better Shepherd than One Who has been a sheep? Imagine the rejoicing in John the Baptist's heart when he pointed and said, in effect, "Look! There is the Lamb of God that will take away the sins of the world!" (John 1:29)

A shepherd is never separated from his sheep. He lies down outside the door at night and never leaves, so that he can protect them from all harmful danger.

10 The thief cometh not, but for to steal, and to kill, and to destroy: I am come that they might have life, and that they might have it more abundantly.

11 I am the good shepherd: the good shepherd giveth his life for the sheep.

14 I am the good shepherd, and know my sheep, and am known of mine. (John 10:10,11,14)

Revelation 7:15-17 talks about the Lamb and the Shepherd combination.

15 Therefore are they before the throne of God, and serve him day and night in his temple: and he that sitteth on the throne shall dwell among them.

16 They shall hunger no more, neither thirst any more; neither shall the sun light on them, nor any heat.

17 For the Lamb which is in the midst of the throne shall feed them, and shall lead them

179

unto living fountains of waters: and God shall wipe away all tears from their eyes. (Revelation 7:15-17)

Jesus, the Lamb, is your Shepherd! Do you see Who Jehovah Rohi is, inside you? He knows how you feel, because He walked in the flesh. He has looked out from your eyes, heard from your ears, and felt all that you feel. He knows exactly how to lead you. He is inside of you specifically to feed you, lead you, and keep you from trouble.

Don't ever say that you do not know God's will. **Jehovah Rohi lives within you,** and the Bible says His Spirit will lead you into **all** truth. The truth of His perfect will. Hold fast to what the Word says.

One time, God spoke to Elijah and said, "Go speak to Ahab." Elijah had been very concerned for Israel, because they had turned their backs on the Lord, and began worshipping idols. Ahab's nasty wife, Jezebel, had led the entire nation into worshipping a certain idol named Baal.

God told Elijah, "I told My people that if they worshipped idols, I would close the heavens and it wouldn't rain. I want you to take this message to Ahab"

Elijah took that promise to Ahab...but then he ran away.

What happened?

The Word of the Lord came to him, and God took him to a little brook called Cherith, where God fed Him morning and evening, supplying him with food brought by the ravens. After a while, it was time for Elijah to move again.

God told him, "This brook is drying up from the drought, and I have plans for you to bring My people out of idolatry."

Elijah ended up in Zarapheth, where Ahab and Jezebel lived, and the Word of the Lord came to him again, saying,

"Tell Ahab to bring all the prophets of Baal to the top of Mount Carmel. Let them build an altar, and you rebuild the altar that has been torn down. Then, let the God Who answers by fire be God. Let's settle this once and for all!"

The prophets of Baal liked the idea, because Baal was supposedly a "god of fire."

26 And they took the bullock which was given them, and they dressed it, and called on the name of Baal from morning even until noon, saying, O Baal, hear us. But there was no voice, nor any that answered. And they leaped upon the altar which was made.

27 And it came to pass at noon, that Elijah mocked them, and said, Cry aloud: for he is a god; either he is talking, or he is pursuing, or he is in a journey, or peradventure he sleepeth, and must be awaked.

28 And they cried aloud, and cut themselves after their manner with knives and lancets, till the blood gushed out upon them. (1st Kings 18:26-28)

There was Elijah, taunting the prophets of Baal, "Your god must be on vacation. Maybe he's deaf, maybe he's taking a nap." Then, Elijah repaired the altar which had been torn down. He put a bullock on it, and prayed a simple prayer.

36b LORD God of Abraham, Isaac, and of Is-
rael, let it be known this day that thou art God
in Israel, and that I am thy servant, and that I
have done all these things at thy word.

37 Hear me, O LORD, hear me, that this people
may know that thou art the Lord God, and that
thou hast turned their heart back again.

38 Then the fire of the LORD fell, and con-
sumed the burnt sacrifice, and the wood, and
the stones, and the dust, and licked up the
water that was in the trench. (1st Kings 18:36b-
38)

Not just the sacrifice, but the wood, stones, dust, and nearby water were **consumed** in God's fire!

Why?

Jehovah Rohi was leading and guiding Elijah, just as He desires to lead and guide you.

After this happened, the Israelites all repented before Jehovah God. Elijah told them to kill all of Baal's prophet's, and they obeyed. Then he began to pray on that mountain, and the Lord opened the heavens and sent the Israelites **rain,** after the drought which had continued throughout their time of idolatry.

The hand of the Lord came upon Elijah, and he ran in the Lord's strength into Jezreel, before the chariot of Ahab, in that rain. When he arrived at Jezreel, bad news arrived too. Jezebel had sent Elijah a note saying that she intended to kill him, since he had killed her prophets. Instead of waiting for the Word from the Lord, Elijah ran away.

Jehovah Rohi had been wonderfully leading Elijah by His Word, but Elijah missed it, and ran from what God had for him. After running away, he prayed to die, being so depressed about his failure. Then Jehovah Rohi caused Elijah to sleep, and sent an angel to feed him. After Elijah ate a second time, Jehovah Rohi told him to go to Mount Horeb, forty days away. **Horeb** means "fresh inspiration," and that is exactly what the Lord intended for Elijah. He was directing Elijah into good things.

When Elijah arrived at Mount Horeb, God taught him a lesson about **how he could trust in Jehovah Rohi's guidance.** Elijah walked into a cave, and suddenly a tremendous wind rushed through. Elijah thought, "That's God!" God said, "No." Then a big earthquake shook the ground. Elijah thought, "That's God!" God said, "No." After that, God caused fire to come. Elijah thought, "That's God!" God said, "No." Then He said, "Elijah, **I am the still, small voice. I am the Word inside you, and that is how I will guide you. Quit looking for huge, outward manifestations. Just look to my Word inside of you.**"

The psalmist said, *Thy word have I hid in mine heart, that I might not sin against thee.* (Psalms 119:11)

Jehovah was saying, "**I want to lead you with My Word. When you listen to My Word, you won't sin,**Elijah." Then the Lord said, "Elijah, I'm not finished with you yet. I am giving you fresh inspiration up here, showing you how to be led by the Word, and not blow it. Don't worry about Ahab and Jezebel--they're going to die."

Then Elijah was instructed, beautifully, that a man named Elisha would be sent to take over his prophetic ministry, when the Lord was ready to take Elijah home! That was fresh inspiration!

Elijah never blew it again?

Why?

He learned that **Jehovah Rohi was inside him to lead and guide him.** Your image in Jesus is that you're **filled with** the knowledge of His will! You do not have to wonder whether you are in God's will. **He is the Lord, Jehovah your Shepherd. He promised to lead you into ALL truth.** That's good news today.

Jehovah Rohi - Isn't it a comfort to know the Lord as Jehovah Rohi? And it's great to know He desires to keep us in His perfect will. By knowing Him as your **Jehovah Rohi,** you can always be confident enough to say, **"Surely goodness and mercy shall follow me all the days of my life!" When you need assurance of His guidance,** there are plenty of scriptures which will beautifully direct you.

20 Now the God of peace, that brought again from the dead our Lord Jesus, that great shepherd of the sheep, through the blood of the everlasting covenant,

21 Make you perfect in every good work to do his will, working in you that which is well-pleasing in his sight, through Jesus Christ; to whom be glory for ever and ever, Amen. (Hebrews 13:20-21)

For ye were as sheep going astray; but are now returned unto the Shepherd and Bishop of your souls. (1st Peter 2:25)

And when the chief Shepherd shall appear, ye shall receive a crown of glory that fadeth not away. (1st Peter 5:4)

14 I am the good shepherd, and know my sheep, and am known of mine.

15 As the Father knoweth me, even so know I the Father: and I lay down my life for the sheep.

16 And other sheep I have, which are not of this fold: them also I must bring, and they shall hear my voice; and there shall be one fold, and one shepherd. (John 10:14-16)

185

Chapter 12

JEHOVAH SHAMMAH

Jehovah Shammah Means **Jehovah is there.** This name is first found in Ezekiel 48:35, where Ezekiel speaks of a city.

...and the name of the city from that day shall be, **The LORD is there.** (Ezekiel 48:35)

This is the Lord's promise and pledge to His people that His presence would be with them. Let's examine why this name was found in this particular place in Ezekiel, for the first time.

Ezekiel was prophesying, probably while in captivity in Babylon. At the time, Israel was falling continually into sin, and Jerusalem was about to go under. Everything was bad news!

So the Lord led Ezekiel to prophesy about a new temple, a temple such as the Lord's people had never had before--so staggeringly beautiful that it would be far beyond any other temple they had seen. Then, when Ezekiel prophesied about this temple, he said, **"The presence of the Lord will be there."**

The people loved Jerusalem and the temple. Now that the temple there had been destroyed, they were full of sorrow, in Babylonian captivity. Reflecting upon their sorrow, they hung their harps upon willow trees, crying out, "How shall we sing Jehovah's song in a strange land?"

We cannot sing of joy in a strange land, because we are captive. Psalms 137:5-6 shows their love for Jerusalem.

5 If I forget thee, O Jerusalem, let my right hand forget her cunning.

6 If I do not remember thee, let my tongue cleave to the roof of my mouth; if I prefer not Jerusalem above my chief joy. (Psalms 137:5-6)

Ezekiel's prophecy brought his people great consolation and hope for restoration of their land. This was Jehovah's pledge of his presence, in a glorious way that they could not imagine.

Israel, however, was still hung up on having a natural presence of God which they could perceive through their senses. But God's presence was not just an article which they could hang up in a temple. He has always wanted His presence to be so much more than that. The first time God's presence is recorded is in the Garden of Eden.

And they heard the voice of the LORD God walking in the garden in the cool of the day. (Genesis 3:8)

Why has God always desired to have his presence with His people? He desires their fellowship. God, Who had placed man, his creation, in a beautiful garden, came down and walked and talked with them. The presence of God was there, because He wanted their presence with Himself. **Jehovah Shammah wants to have fellowship with you** That's what He is all about. He is present and alive in you--**He is there.**

But the presence and fellowship which existed in the Garden of Eden did not last between the Lord and His people, because Adam sinned. The Word of God does not say that His presence left Adam. It says that Adam left God. Adam hid behind a tree, after willfully sinning.

When God came to visit with him, He said, "Adam, Adam where are you?"

Of course, God is all-knowing and He knew where Adam was. God knew that Adam was hiding, because of the sin which separated him from his Creator.

But that did not stop God from wanting fellowship with His creation. He still took every possible opportunity to continue that fellowship. He walked with Enoch, talked to Abraham, calling him "friend," and He communed with Moses.

One day, God spoke to Moses, saying,

And let them make me a sanctuary; that I may dwell among them. (Exodus 25:8)

"I want to fellowship with them, as well as you, Moses. I want My presence to be with others, by dwelling among them."

At this time, God's people were in tents and on the move. Everything had to be portable, and it wasn't very beautiful or glamorous.

But God said, "I want My presence to be in the tent, too. If you are a pilgrim, I want to be a pilgrim with you. If you live in a tent, I will abide there with you."

God fellowships with you, wherever you are! So the presence of God came down as a pillar of cloud and a pillar of fire over the holy of holies, and He occupied a tent with tent dwellers.

Are you out in the "wilderness?" Do you feel like you're running around in a dry desert? Well, God was saying, "If that is where you are, that's where I want to be, too."

He stated it wonderfully in Exodus.

And there I will meet with thee, and I will commune with thee.... (Exodus 25:22)

He is **there** with you, communing with you, because He is your **Jehovah Shammah.**

Finally, the day came when the Israelites went into the promised Land. All the old people had died in the wilderness, but their children entered the land.

When they went in, it only took six and one half years to take the land! They settled down with their own land, trees, crops and homes, and God told King Solomon, "Build Me a temple."

Since the people were now living in houses rather than tents, God desired a house, too.

So God dwelled in the elegant, rich temple which was built by Solomon. There, He continued in fellowship with His people. His presence was there.

First Kings 8:11 describes one of the wonderful worship services held in Solomon's temple.

So that the priests could not stand to minister because of the cloud: for the glory of the LORD had filled the house of the LORD. (1st Kings 8:11)

The presence of God Himself came in and filled up the temple.

Why?

God wanted to be where His people were. He wanted to abide in their praise.

But that did not last, either, because Solomon's temple was temporary, just as the garden and the tabernacle were.

So God said, "I'm going to have to deal with the people, because they have forsaken Me, even though My presence has been with them. They've left Me, and they are following idols."

Ezekiel had a vision about the presence of God leaving the temple, which it did. He saw it lifting from the holy of holies, hovering over the city's wall, and then lifting and rising into the sky, away from them.

God's presence left the temple. It was tragic to the people. They were carried into Babylonian captivity for seventy years, and there they had their fill of idolatry.

They never touched idols again after that. Still, the Lord had told them, "I'll never leave you. Even though you have left Me, I will not leave you."

Just as Jeremiah had prophesied, finally after seventy years of captivity, the Israelites returned to their land of promise. It is really touching how God never gives up on us. He continually gives us opportunities to be right with Him, in His presence.

When the children of Israel returned to the Promised Land, they built another temple, which was called Zerubbabel's temple. Compared to Solomon's temple, it was very crude. The people were poor, and they had to scrape things together just to be able to build at all.

15 And this house was finished on the third day of the month Adar, which was in the sixth year of the reign of Darius the king.

16 And the children of Israel, the priests, and the Levites and the rest of the children of the captivity, kept the dedication of the house of God with joy. (Ezra 6:15-16)

When the old men saw this temple and remembered the grandness of Solomon's temple, they cried. This temple could never compare to the previous temple's standards. But the young people rejoiced, because they didn't know what it was to have any other temple. They were just glad to have one!

The Bible says, **the poorness of this structure was not what determined God's presence there. His presence still rested upon it.**

No matter where you are, God is there. He is Jehovah Shammah, keeping His pledge. He will never leave nor forsake you, because His presence is within you.

Years later, when King Herod saw Zerubbabel's temple, he thought, "How crude!" So he rebuilt the temple and added wealth and splendor to it.

But the drawback was that Herod wasn't building it for the presence of God. He hated God. Herod wanted only to build a name for himself. There was no shekinah glory.

When Jesus came to this temple, He ministered in the outer court, and told the people, "You have made the temple into a den of thieves."

Where was God's presence at this time? The Bible says that God was in His Son, Jesus Christ. God's presence moved into the bodily temple of His son.

To wit, that God was in Christ, reconciling the world unto himself, not imputing their trespasses unto them; and hath committed unto us the word of reconciliation. (2nd Corinthians 5:19)

No wonder Jesus told the Pharisees,

19...Destroy this temple, and in three days I will raise it up.

20 Then said the Jews, Forty and six years was this temple in building, and wilt thou rear it up in three days?

21 But he spake of the temple of his body. (John 2:19-21)

Colossians 2:9 says, *"For in him dwelleth all the fulness of the Godhead bodily,* and one of Jesus' names is **Emmanuel,** meaning "**God with us.**" He dwelt within Jesus then--and He still does, now.

All of the man-made temples were very short-lived. God did not stay in the garden. The tabernacle was substituted with a temple. Solomon's temple was destroyed by Nebuchadnezzar. Zerubbabel's temple was destroyed by Herod. And finally, sinful people crucified Jesus.

Now, where was the presence of God? After Jesus' resurrection, those who received Him as Savior and Lord became His temples! **You are now the temple of God. When you invited Jesus into your heart, Jehovah Shammah came in.**

> *Know ye not that ye are the temple of God, and that the Spirit of God dwelleth in you?* (1st Corinthian 3:16)

> *...for ye are the temple of the living God; as God hath said, I will dwell in them, and walk in them; and I will be their God, and they shall be my people.* (2nd Corinthians 6:16)

Colossians 1:27 says, *"which is Christ **in** you, the hope of glory."* You might say, "But Marilyn, I'm going to die! I am not here forever--if it is appointed unto men once to die, then where is the temple?"

Yes, your body is temporary. It will be destroyed by death, the last enemy, unless Jesus comes before that time. But the Lord has something even better in store for you after you die. He said He will always be with you.

> *For we know that if our earthly house of this tabernacle were dissolved, we have a building of God, an house not made with hands, eternal in the heavens.* (2nd Corinthians 5:1)

God is saying, "Don't worry. I have a temple. I'll always have a place for my presence with you, but this time it is eternal, in heaven. You will be in My presence forever."

In the beginning, God came down to earth to fellowship with man. But now, we have ended up with man going up to dwell with God forever. How good God is! He unfolds His beautiful plan and picture—**Jehovah Shammah.**

The Bible tells us that from the very beginning, God wanted His presence felt. He once spoke to Moses, saying, "My presence shall go with you, and I will give you rest." Moses wouldn't go anywhere if he didn't know that God's presence went with him! But you don't have to worry about that. He is **in** you!

In all their affliction he was afflicted, and the angel of his presence saved them: in his love and in his pity he redeemed them; and he bare them, and carries them all the days of old. (Isaiah 63:9)

The Lord's presence is what has saved you. His presence is there to feel what you feel, and take you through each situation. It is what you need in every moment of your life.

David loved Jehovah's presence. He even wanted to build a house for His presence, but the Lord would not allow it.

The presence of God is wonderful, and His glory goes everywhere you go. **Glory** always relates to "shekinah," which means "to live in you."

That is why God said that He would dwell **in** you. He said, *"I will live in you, walk in you, and be your God, and you will be my people"* (2nd Corinthians 6:16).

Where does God's presence go?

It goes where you go. When is His presence with you? **When you sleep, when you wake up, when you walk, work or eat--no matter where you go, JEHOVAH IS THERE!**

21 In whom all the building fitly framed together groweth unto an holy temple in the Lord:

22 In whom ye also are builded together for an habitation of God through the Spirit. (Ephesians 2:21-22)

The Lord is building us, the Church, into His most glorious temple ever. We will all be one in Him, living with Him in an eternal dwelling place. No matter where you or I could go, **He is Jehovah Shammah!** We are just traveling through this life on earth, taking His presence to others. But we can say, just as the apostle Paul said, "My citizenship is in heaven."

1 And I saw a new heaven and a new earth: for the first heaven and the first earth were passed away; and there was no more sea.

2 And I John saw the holy city, new Jerusalem, coming down from God out of heaven, prepared as a bride adorned for her husband.

3 And I heard a great voice out of heaven saying, Behold, the tabernacle of God is with men, and he will dwell with them, and they will be his people, and God himself shall be with them, and be their God. (Revelation 21:1-3)

That beautiful city has precious stone, a crystal river, delectable food, and a tree of life with leaves for the healing of the nations. It is full of Jesus' light, love and holiness. It is full of worship, joy and safety.

There will be no curse, no adversary, no defilement or sorrow. Every wicked doer will be cut off, and Jehovah's glory will be manifested in fullness.

Together, we'll say,

Blessing, and honour, and glory, and power, be unto him that sitteth upon the throne and unto the Lamb for ever and ever (Revelation 5:13).

Why?

His eternal presence will be forever there, WITH US. FOREVER we will dwell with JEHOVAH SHAMMAH!

Not only is Jehovah there, however--he is **here**. He is with you, and in you. He will never leave you nor forsake you, not even for a second! When you are surrounded with difficult circumstances, or when all is going well, look to His presence inside you. It's abiding within you.

Are you in a tabernacle? A wilderness? He's there. Are you in a garden? He is there. Are you in a temple? He is there. Jehovah is in you, walking and talking. His being is there. Don't ever forget it. When you look in the mirror, say, **Jesus is in me, the hope of glory!**

Jehovah Shammah - Wherever you go, the Lord goes with you. What a privilege it is to live in the sweet presence of the Lord each day. Study these scriptures. Realize His pledge to abide with you forever--it is His promise to complete what He has begun in your life. Truly, **Jehovah is there!**

9 Therefore my heart is glad, and my glory rejoiceth: my flesh also shall rest in hope.

11 Thou wilt shew me the path of life; in thy presence is fulness of joy; at thy right hand there are pleasures for evermore. (Psalms 16:9,11)

Know ye not that ye are the temple of God, and that the Spirit of God dwelleth in you? (1st Corinthians 3:16)

19 Go ye therefore, and teach all nations, baptizing them in the name of the Father, and of the Son, and of the Holy Ghost:

20 Teaching them to observe all things whatsoever I have commanded you: and, lo, I am with you alway, even unto the end of the world. (Matthew 28:19-20)

19 Now therefore ye are no more strangers and foreigners, but fellowcitizens with the saints, and of the household of God;

20 And are built upon the foundation of the apostles and prophets, Jesus Christ himself being the chief corner stone;

21 In whom all the building fitly framed together groweth unto an holy temple in the

Lord:

22 In whom ye also are builded together for an habitation of God through the Spirit. (Ephesians 2:19-22)

Receive Jesus Christ as
Lord and Savior of Your Life

The Bible says, "that if thou shalt confess with thy mouth the Lord Jesus, and shalt believe in thine heart that God hath raised him from the dead, thou shalt be saved. For with the heart man believeth unto righteousness; and with the mouth confession is made unto salvation" (Romans 10:9-10).

To receive Jesus Christ as Lord and Savior of your life, sincerely pray this prayer from your heart:

Dear Jesus,

I believe that You died for me and that You rose again on the third day. I confess to You that I am a sinner and that I need Your love and forgiveness. Come into my life, forgive my sins and give me eternal life. I confess You now as my Lord. Thank You for my salvation!

Signed _____

Date _____

Write to us. We will send you information to help you with your new life in Christ. Marilyn Hickey Ministries • P.O. Box 17340 • Denver, CO 80217

BOOKS BY MARILYN HICKEY
ORDER BLANK

BOOK TITLE	CODE	PRICE EACH	QUAN.	TOTAL PRICE
Beat Tension	BK I	$ .75		
Change Your Life	BK V	.75		
Conquering Setbacks	BK C	.75		
Dear Marilyn	BK KK	6.95		
Divorce Is Not The Answer	BK D	2.95		
Egypt Revisited In Prophecy	BK H	1.95		
Experience Long Life	BK Z	.75		
Fasting & Prayer	BK W	.75		
Fear Free, Faith Filled	BK U	3.25		
Freedom From Bondages	BK HH	4.95		
Gift Wrapped Fruit	BK O	2.00		
God IN You, TO You, And FOR You	BK AA	4.95		
God's Benefit: Healing	BK P	.75		
God's Covenant For Your Family	BK S	4.95		
God's RX For A Hurting Heart	BK Q	3.25		
God's Seven Keys To Make You Rich	BK N	.75		
Hold On To Your Dreams	BK Y	.75		
How To Be A Mature Christian	BK II	5.95		
How To Become More Than A Conqueror	BK K	.75		
How To Win Friends	BK J	.75		
I Can Be Born Again	BK EE	.75		
I Can Dare To Be An Achiever	BK FF	.75		
Keys To Healing Rejection	BK M	.75		
Motivational Gifts	BK X	3.50		
#1 Key to Success—Meditation	BK BB	2.50		
Power Of Forgiveness	BK B	.75		
Receive the Evidence of the Spirit-filled Life	BK DD	4.95		
Renew Your Mind	BK E	.75		
Signs in the Heavens	BK GG	4.95		
Smooth Out Your Rough Edges	BK JJ	7.95		
Speak The Word	BK A	.75		
Standing In The Gap	BK L	.75		
Treading With Angels	BK F	2.95		
Winning Over Weight	BK T	.75		
Women Of The Word	BK G	.75		
Your Miracle Source	BK R	2.50		

Prices subject to change without notice
Please Print:

TOTAL _____

Name Miss Mrs. Mr. _____

Address _____

City _____ State _____ Zip _____

Phone (_____) _____

Circle One:

VISA   MasterCard   ___ — ___ — ___

Please print number   Expiration date

_____
Signature

For information regarding Marilyn Hickey's monthly Bible reading program, you may write:
TIME WITH HIM • P.O. Box 17340 • Denver, CO 80217

MARILYN HICKEY MINISTRIES

is based in God's call
"To Cover the Earth with His Word."

We invite you to share in any of the following ministry programs:

☐ Please send me your complimentary, monthly magazine
TIME WITH HIM, which includes daily devotionals,
teaching articles, and ministry updates.
☐ Please send me Marilyn Hickey's latest product catalog.

LET US JOIN OUR FAITH WITH YOURS FOR YOUR
PRAYER NEEDS.
  * Call our 24-hour prayer LIFE LINE with any problem or
pain. Receive prayers of agreement and encouragement.
Learn God's solutions to problems. (303) 777-5029.

  * Send your written prayer requests to Marilyn: _____
_____
_____
_____

MARILYN HICKEY MINISTRIES
P.O. BOX 17340
DENVER, CO 80217